BARNSTORMING BABE

A SLUGGER'S BUMPY TREK ACROSS SMALL-TOWN AMERICA

BARNSTORMING
BABE

A SLUGGER'S
BUMPY TREK
ACROSS
SMALL-TOWN
AMERICA

TIMOTHY GROVER

www.BookpressPublishing.com

Published in Des Moines, Iowa, by:

Bookpress Publishing
P.O. Box 71532, Des Moines, IA 50325
www.BookpressPublishing.com

Publisher's Cataloging-in-Publication Data

Names: Grover, Timothy, author.
Title: Barnstorming Babe : a slugger's bumpy trek across small-town America / Timothy Grover.
Description: Des Moines, IA: BookPress Publishing, 2023.
Identifiers: LCCN: 2022914945 | ISBN: 978-1-947305-53-3
Subjects: LCSH Ruth, Babe, 1895-1948. | Meusel, Robert William. | Baseball players--Biography. | New York Yankees (Baseball team)--History--20th century. | BISAC BIOGRAPHY & AUTOBIOGRAPHY / Sports | SPORTS & RECREATION / Baseball / History
Classification: LCC GV865.R8 .G76 2023 | DDC 796.357/092--dc23

First Edition
Printed in the United States of America
10 9 8 7 6 5 4 3 2 1

This book is dedicated to my wife, Deb.
Thanks for being my rock and my
soulmate for over forty years.
Love ya Babe!

ACKNOWLEDGMENTS

When I began researching Babe Ruth's barnstorming visits into Iowa in the 1920s, I never dreamed it would evolve into a book. There's a long list of people who collaborated, contributed, and inspired me on this journey.

First of all, thanks to Bookpress Publishing for believing in my project. Susan Holden Martin did a brilliant job of editing, and thanks also to the rest of the Bookpress team!

For background information about the Perry ballgame, thanks to Rod Stanley at the Dexter Historical Museum in Dexter, Iowa, and the staff at the Forest Park Museum in Perry, Iowa. Darcy Maulsby provided a great photo of the Perry ballclub, and thanks to Lois Smith and Valerie Van Kooten from the Pella Historical Society for the Pella Meteors team photo.

Debbie Joramo supplied the Sleepy Eye photo, which included the Len Youngman photo bomb. I hope to visit Sleepy Eye, Minnesota, sometime and see the field Babe and Bob actually played on. Thanks to Blake Huppert, a brilliant television reporter, for his 2016 Len Youngman profile.

I'm grateful to Rose Speirs at Deadwood History Inc. and Margaret Ward Masias at the Pueblo Historical Society for their contributions. Special thanks to Dr. Raymond Doswell at the Negro League Museum in Kansas City; I was honored to meet you.

For feedback on my early drafts and encouragement during the process, thanks to Michael Diver, my brother Tony Grover, and my son Matt Grover. Thanks also to the Des Moines Writer's Workshop for their encouragement.

There are many special people over the years who have helped me believe in myself and focus on my goals. Special shout-outs to Valerie, Kate, Arthurine, and the coaches at Changing Course; also to Barbara Sher and Barbara Winter for inspiring me to overcome my doubts and follow my dreams.

I've been blessed to have an amazing family, starting with my parents Max and Charlotte Grover. They both love history and continue to stay curious about nearly everything. Mom taught me the joy of reading, and Dad showed me how to tell great stories.

Thanks to my daughter Emily Bainter for her intelligence, insights, and humor. She and her husband Jesse have also blessed us with two incredible grandsons, Isaac and Owen. They fill our hearts with joy and give us hope for the future.

Daughter Abby, thank you for the brightness and inspiration you bring into our lives. You challenge us to approach the world differently in your independent, loving way.

Matt, thanks for being the athlete I never was! I appreciate your feedback on my writing and love our baseball times together. Congrats on your successful business and in marrying Lauren, she's the perfect woman to keep you in line.

And I need to mention my nephew, Kellin Vogel. He's the biggest young sports fan I know—and appreciates baseball history. Love ya buddy!

Most of all, thank you to my beautiful wife and best friend Deb. I was enthralled by your smile the first time I saw you. We've been through a lot since 1979, and you've always stuck with me. I appreciate your organization and hard work. Enjoy your well-earned retirement!

Finally, I offer humble thanks and blessings to my readers. Stay curious, ask questions, and be kind.

Prologue

I've loved baseball and history for a long time. My brother and I often drifted off to sleep listening to Minnesota Twins broadcasts on WHO radio from Des Moines, a thousand cornfields distant. We heard Merle Harmon and Herb Carneal describe Harmon Killebrew's jaw-dropping blasts and Rod Carew stealing home yet again (he did it seven times in 1969!).

Besides the TV drama of the Miracle Mets and watching Hank Aaron break Babe Ruth's home run record, I have some great eyewitness memories:

- Seeing Ernie Banks pinch hit at Wrigley in 1970. He grounded out, but we still cheered.

• Being on the Heritage Cablevision crew and running centerfield camera for Iowa Cubs telecasts in the 1980s. In one game, the Cubs' third baseman Wade Rowdon hit four homers.

• My first Twins game at Target Field with my son Matt, son-in-law Jesse, and nephew Ryan. The pre-COVID, 2019 Bomba Squad delivered for us.

About ten years ago, I received a book written by baseball historian Bill Jenkinson with an intriguing title: *The Year Babe Ruth Hit 104 Home Runs*. The book methodically chronicles every career home run Ruth hit. He includes regular season dates, who was pitching, distances, and where the ball landed. And he included spring training, exhibition, post-season, and barnstorming games. I've lived in Iowa my whole life, and I had no idea Babe Ruth actually played here—three times—during the 1920s.

Following a tumultuous 1922 season and a terrible World Series, Babe Ruth and Bob Meusel undertook a barnstorming journey that crisscrossed eight Great Plains states in less than three weeks. Afterward, Ruth told reporters they sometimes slept "…all night on the floor of a day coach on a jerkwater railroad…." Their first game was in Perry, Iowa, about 45 minutes northwest of my home in suburban Des Moines.

What would it have been like a century ago to hear that Babe Ruth would be playing in your hometown? Especially when you lived in a random farm town—not even a county seat! I imagine moon-eyed boys, nervous civic underwriters, and cocky town ball pitchers bragging about how they'll strike out the Bambino.

What caused the barnstormers to pick Sleepy Eye, Minnesota, over the Twin Cities? How did local fans and newspapers react to seeing major league ballplayers? How did Babe and Bob contend with the grind of playing on seventeen different fields in seventeen consecutive days—with some towns over 400 miles apart?

Here's the story about Barnstorming Babe Ruth's amazing and sometimes bumpy trek across small-town America.

Babe is Struck Out by a Spitball

Having tripled his first time up, the planet's most famous athlete ambled to the plate on a blustery October afternoon. As dust devils swirled, he worked the count to two and two. The next pitch took a strange dip as it reached the plate. The burly left-handed batter took a mighty swing. And he missed.

Five days earlier, the legendary Babe Ruth had played right field for the losing Yankees in the 1922 World Series. He had disappointed everyone but the New York Giants fans, batting an anemic .118—by far, the worst batting average of a position player on either team. It helped John McGraw's club sweep the Yankees for a second consecutive year.

The World Series capped a bizarre 1922 season for the Bambino. Suspended for the first six weeks, Ruth slumped after being activated in late May. His frustrations led to several more suspensions during the summer. Despite those challenges, he finished his abbreviated 110-game season, hitting .315 with 35 homers. Those were impressive stats for any everyday player. But the numbers hadn't met the expectations of fickle Yankee fans or Babe Ruth himself.

That previous Sunday, the Polo Grounds in New York hosted 38,551 fans for the Series finale. Today, 800 antsy Iowans shivered in the Dallas County bleachers. They had each swapped a hard-earned silver dollar expecting Babe Ruth to blast a baseball deep into a fenceless right field where

Babe missing a pitch in Perry, Iowa, on October 13, 1922.

Photo Credit: Des Moines Tribune, October 14, 1922

it would roll all the way to Ames. Instead, a Dutchman named Versteeg struck him out.

Baseball had outlawed the spitball two years earlier. That didn't stop the Pella Meteors' pitcher from coughing into his hand before notching a strikeout. The Bambino muttered a curse at the "bush league spitballer" as he wandered back to the dugout. But Babe Ruth got revenge his next time up. Like other aspects of his life, his response was unconventional, entertaining, and outside the lines.

And it all happened on a Friday afternoon in central Iowa.

A Rare Chance to See the Bambino

In an era that revolutionized the game almost overnight, baseball's popularity exploded in the early 1920s. Factories sponsored semi-pro teams, sometimes hiring workers exclusively for their pitching skills. Dairy farmers swapped coveralls for wool uniforms on Sundays, playing against rival towns after church. If city parks or high school fields weren't available, teams played in cow pastures. Kids played pickup games on front lawns, parking lots, and in back alleys.

In rural America, major league fans relied on newspapers for game summaries, box scores, and offseason trade rumors. The first radio station—KDKA in Pittsburgh—began transmitting in November 1920. However, fewer than one percent of farmers had electricity, and not many owned battery-powered radios. Besides, only 30 stations were broadcasting in the United States by the end of 1921.

In the Great Plains, attending a major league ballgame required traveling on a coal-fired, steam-driven passenger train to either St. Louis or Chicago. A few well-heeled folks owned a Model T or maybe a fancier "motorcar" from one of the several hundred boutique companies competing against Henry Ford. But a large swath of rural America had yet to evolve from the horse-and-buggy era; most early roadways were ungraded and unpaved. After a rain, roads turned to muck, and travel became difficult.

During the First World War, many farming operations had expanded to meet the global food crisis, and farmers were paid well for their efforts. But as the war ended and Europe began to recover economically, commodity prices crashed quickly. In Minnesota, between 1919 and 1920, corn tumbled from $1.30 per bushel to 47 cents. Wheat and hog prices followed a similar trend.

Fortunately for hardscrabble fans, thousands of affordable and accessible exhibition games were played by major leaguers in the early 1900s. After spring training, some teams played one another in smaller cities as they headed north to their home ballparks. For example, the Brooklyn Dodgers could play the New York Yankees in Savannah, then play them again the following afternoon in Wilmington. On off-days during the regular season, big leaguers sometimes competed against minor league farm clubs for extra money. And after the World Series, many players did some post-season barnstorming tours.

In retrospect, some game locations boggled the mind. Imagine being a cattle rancher in October 1922, living near Pratt, Kansas. The nearest city is Wichita, 80 miles east. You shake your head in disbelief at the front page of the Pratt Daily Tribune and think to yourself, "BABE RUTH will be playing in PRATT next Thursday? Here in PRATT? Jiminy Christmas!"

America's biggest superstar blasting home runs into empty skies against small-town pitchers? It may be inconceivable today, but Babe Ruth and Yankee teammate Bob Meusel kicked off an exhausting eighteen-game, 3,300-mile barnstorming tour only three days after the 1922 World Series. Long before Learjets, Winnebagos, and limousines, Ruth said they traveled primarily on "jerkwater railroads."

Other than several 1919 California exhibitions and a few spring training games in the Deep South, this would be the first time Babe Ruth played baseball west of St Louis. Bill Jenkinson writes, "It is difficult for us to understand the significance of these events. We now have ESPN and other television networks showing us the highlights of every game...to actually see Babe Ruth hit a baseball was an experience that no one ever forgot."

His 1922 midwestern small-town barnstorming tour kicked off on Friday, October 13th, in Perry, home to 5,642 central Iowans.

The Making of a Legend

Nearly 75 years after his death, 90 years after his final game, and a century after his "Small-Town America Tour," ESPN writers chose Babe Ruth as the greatest baseball player of all time. Famed for his legendary home runs, the southpaw pitched brilliantly in his early years with a 94-46 career record.

Rising from humble beginnings, he was embraced by the working class, the underclass, and the racially marginalized during the Jim Crow era. Babe's showmanship, humor, and genuine love for kids helped restore baseball's soiled reputation after the 1919 Black Sox scandal and rescued it from an uncertain destiny. His personality and marketing savvy shaped American mythology, popular culture, and professional sports in ways recognizable a century later. He made a lot of money along the way—and spent even more.

Born to abusive German immigrants in 1895, George Herman Ruth, Jr. was raised in squalid conditions. Today, Baltimore's Inner Harbor area is a tourism mecca, featuring a con-vention center and stunning ballparks for both Major League Baseball's Baltimore Orioles and the NFL's Ravens. But back in the 1890s, untreated stockyard waste seeped into the shallow harbor. Tides and geography also caused the estuary to retain much of Baltimore's

George Ruth junior, age seven (at right), soon after arriving at St. Mary's Industrial School in 1902. On the left is Ruth's friend John DeTullio.

Photo Credit: Wikimedia Commons

sewage. Nearby rail and coal yards for the B & O Railroad filled the air with smoke and dust. Rampant disease and malnutrition caused the area's infant mortality rate to reach 10 percent in 1900. In this sorry neighborhood, little George Ruth spent his formative years.

Pregnant with George Jr. when she married, the former Catherine Schamberger would give birth to eight children. Only two survived to adulthood. Katie, as she was known, reportedly dealt with multiple chronic physical and psychological ailments. She never had a loving relationship with her only son. George Sr. divorced her in 1906 on the grounds of alcoholism and adultery; he was granted sole custody of little George and his sister Mamie.

Moving frequently within the same few blocks of the noisy B&O Railroad yard, George Sr. worked grueling hours as a saloon keeper on property now belonging to Camden Yards, home of the Baltimore Orioles.

Lacking an intimate connection with either parent, George Jr. got into trouble early and often. By age seven, he

St. Mary's catcher Babe Ruth chats with a teammate in 1912.

Photo Credit: Wikimedia Commons

skipped school, chewed tobacco, shoplifted, and chucked rocks at delivery men. Harsh beatings from his father didn't curb his behavior. Exasperated, George Sr. arranged for a neighborhood cop to escort the youngster to St. Mary's Industrial School, a nearby facility for delinquent children. There, a monk named Brother Matthias took a special interest in the unruly lad. He provided the emotional support and stability the boy desperately needed. Large and strong (hitting fungo balls with one hand), he was a tough but fair disciplinarian. A fine athlete himself, Matthias channeled the boy's energy into learning baseball. "And how to think," Ruth later said.

Babe Ruth (center) with his father, George Herman Ruth, Sr., tend bar in Baltimore in 1915. The elder Ruth owned several Baltimore saloons in the current area of Camden Yards, home of the Baltimore Orioles.

Photo Credit: Wikimedia Commons

By his late teens, George had developed into a superb left-handed pitcher. His skill led Baltimore Orioles owner Jack Dunn to offer him a $600 contract to join his minor league club in 1914. Teammates nicknamed the moon-faced rookie "Babe."

Later that year, Dunn sold Ruth and two other players to the Boston Red Sox for $25,000. Babe won his major league pitching debut two days later against Cleveland, 4-3. But, stacked with a stellar pitching staff, the Sox optioned Babe to the minors. He helped lead the Providence Grays to an International League championship. Called back up to Boston, Ruth pitched in four games, finished with a 2-1 record, and got his first two big-league hits.

A photo from Babe's first game with the minor league Baltimore Orioles. Taken in Fayetteville, North Carolina, on March 7, 1914. He hit a home run in that game.

Photo Credit: General Negative Collection, State Archives of North Carolina, Raleigh, NC.

A Brilliant Career with the Red Sox

Ruth pitched brilliantly as a starter from 1915 through 1917. He won 18 games in 1915, following up with a 23-12 record and 1.75 ERA in 1916. In the 1916 World Series, Babe threw fourteen scoreless innings against the Brooklyn Robins. By the end of 1917, his career pitching record was 67-34, with a .299 career batting average.

Ruth had a 13-7 pitching record in 1918 as he began transitioning to the outfield. Hitting .300, his 11 homers tied Tilly Walker for the American League lead. In his next 13 seasons, Ruth would either lead or tie for the most home runs 11 times.

His talent led the Red Sox to another World Series title in 1918, this time against the Chicago Cubs. Continuing his streak, he pitched nearly 30 more consecutive scoreless

Ruth with other Red Sox pitchers after being called up to Boston in 1915. Left to right: Rube Foster, Carl Mays, Ernie Shore, Babe Ruth, and Dutch Leonard. Combined, they posted a 77-36 record.

Photo Credit: Wikimedia Commons

innings before giving up a run.

In what became his last year in Boston, Babe had an outstanding 1919 campaign. He batted .322, had a 9-5 pitching record, and shattered a major league record with 29 homers. That fall, he embarked on a New England barnstorming tour. He then headed to California, playing several more games and visiting Hollywood.

Ruth eventually became one of the first sports figures to hire an agent. Before then, he and other professional ballplayers met one-on-one with team owners to finalize contracts for the coming season.

Ruth's salary had risen from $3,500 in 1915 to $10,000 by 1919 (worth $142,000 today). Although he had been contracted through 1920 for the same $10,000 salary, Ruth justifiably felt he deserved a hefty raise after his brilliant season. Attempting to renegotiate with Red Sox owner Harry Frazee, the Bambino insisted on $20,000 for 1920. Frazee refused, and his response stunned the Red Sox nation. In early January, he sold Babe Ruth to the despised New York Yankees. They had no problem meeting Babe's $20,000 salary demand.

One thing Harry Frazee loved as much as baseball was show business. He produced several successful Broadway plays and built theaters in Chicago and New York. But when squeezed for venture capital, Frazee often sold or traded his best players to trim payroll.

Brewing magnate and Yankees' owner Jacob Ruppert was a frequent buyer. He gladly purchased the contracts of Red Sox stars like Carl Mays, Ernie Shore, and Dutch Leonard. For Babe Ruth, Frazee received $100,000 cash and a $300,000 personal loan from Ruppert (Frazee was rumored to have used Fenway Park as loan collateral).

Frazee gradually depleted the talent of a once-mighty club. Many former Sox players provided the foundation for a Yankee dynasty. With the sale of Babe Ruth, the legendary "Curse of the Bambino" was born.

The World Series began in 1903. Prior to the sale, New York had failed to make a single championship appearance. In Babe Ruth's 15 years with the Yankees, they competed in seven and won four World Series titles.

In contrast, by 1918, the Boston Red Sox had claimed *five of the first fifteen* World Series championships. They wouldn't win another until 2004—an 86-year drought. Only the Cubs (108 years) waited longer. But the Cubs couldn't blame Harry Frazee!

Evolving from the Dead Ball Era

The period from 1900 through 1920 is referred to as baseball's "dead-ball era" for various reasons. Tight-fisted owners often tried using a single, stained baseball for an entire game, tracking down and retrieving foul balls. As stitching unraveled and balls softened, they became impossible to hit with any impact. Hitters also faced doctored pitches, including tobacco-stained spitballs. Spitballs had been outlawed earlier that season, along with other rules designed to make games safer and more exciting.

Most early 20th-century big-league parks were massive. Before moving to Fenway Park in 1912, the Red Sox played at the Huntington Avenue Grounds, where centerfield was reportedly 635 feet. The deepest centerfield fence in the majors today is 210 feet shorter (Comerica Park in Detroit). With diamonds that large, attempting to consistently hit homers would undoubtedly lead to a short career.

Major league diamonds also didn't have lighting until 1935. That made soiled baseballs even harder to see on cloudy days and late afternoons. With those limitations, game strategy in the early 20th century favored "small ball." Managers emphasized bunting, hit-and-run plays, and aggressive baserunning instead of power-hitting. From 1905 to 1928, Ty Cobb epitomized the dead-ball era player.

On August 16, 1920, Yankee submarine pitcher Carl Mays fatally beaned Cleveland batter Ray Chapman. Witnesses said that although Chapman crowded the plate, he may not have even seen the stained baseball since he didn't attempt to avoid it that dusky afternoon.

After the Chapman tragedy, umpires instantly replaced scuffed and dirty baseballs. It still took MLB until 1971 to require batting helmets.

With revolutionary impact, hitters gained a significant advantage over pitchers. Batting averages skyrocketed, run production soared, and hitters focused more on uppercuts than sacrifice bunts. The changes aligned perfectly with Babe Ruth's 1920 debut in New York. He had a slow start, with five homers in his first 28 games. He then blasted seven in the last week of May and entered June by hitting three in a doubleheader against the Senators. He went on a tear, hitting 30 dingers between July 9th and September 29th. Finishing his 1920 season with 54 round-trippers, Ruth nearly doubled the major league home run record he had set a year earlier.

Babe Ruth's 54 home runs exceeded *the total number of team home runs hit by 14 of the other 15 major league clubs*. Nobody had witnessed anything like it.

Ty Cobb bristled at the emphasis on power. It forever changed *"his"* game. How extreme was the contrast in styles between "small ball" and "power ball"? Cobb had 117 career homers in 24 seasons; Ruth had 114 in *two combined* seasons (1927-28).

Ballplayers and Barnstorming

From the Civil War era into the 1920s, communities wanting to consider themselves cultured and progressive built "opera houses." Found in even small rural towns, opera houses hosted concerts, conventions, and speaking engagements. Visiting politicians sometimes found opera houses weren't available, so they moved their rallies to barns and "barnstormed." The term was soon adapted to describe baseball exhibition tours.

Baseball barnstorming had been common since the 1880s, and players welcomed the off-season income. For average ballplayers, salaries varied little from common working men. And in 1879, major league owners colluded to insert a "reserve clause" statute in player contracts. It prohibited players from signing with other teams for any reason. It effectively gave owners complete financial control over a ballplayer's destiny. This tactic kept salaries artificially lower than a free market would otherwise permit; major leaguers finally achieved free agency in the 1970s.

Expanding their power further, administrators created a new rule in 1914. It prohibited World Series participants from any off-season exhibition tours. The rationale? To prevent championship teams or players from being embarrassed by local amateurs. It didn't apply to major leaguers from lesser teams, who could barnstorm until the snow flew. The rule was arbitrary and seldom enforced. After winning the World Series in 1916 and 1918 with the Red Sox, Babe Ruth played in several exhibitions without repercussion.

Following his 1919 season with Boston and Frazee's refusal to raise his salary, Ruth spent November and December in sunny California. After barnstorming on the West Coast, Babe acted in a cheesy silent movie called *Headin' Home* that portrayed a fictional account of his life.

According to Bill Jenkinson in *The Year Babe Ruth Hit 104 Home Runs*, that experience allowed the Bambino to realize the full extent of his celebrity value. "He was a virtuoso performer who could amaze people with his tremendous power in one moment and then make them laugh in the next instant with his natural comedic instincts."

Ruth earned $15,000 that winter, a significant contrast to the $10,000 he earned during the entire 1919 regular season with the Red Sox.

After Ruth's first season with the Yankees in 1920, he

broke a small wrist bone in an exhibition game. That didn't stop him from joining John McGraw and several New York Giants players for a Cuban barnstorming tour. Jenkinson wrote that the free-spending Babe made "a pile of money," But he may have lost it just as quickly.

According to sportswriter Jane Leavy, during the Cuban trip, Ruth was "locked in a train toilet with Giants' pitcher Rosy Ryan and a gallon of rum on the way back to Havana, where the Babe got stranded, having been swindled out of everything he'd bankrolled by gamblers and con men." According to "exclusive reports," losses ranged "somewhere between $60,000 and $130,000."

After the 1919 regular season, Ruth barnstormed on the west coast and acted in a cheesy movie called *Headin' Home* with actress Ruth Taylor.

Photo Credit: *Exhibitors Herald*, October 16, 1920

A No-Nonsense Judge Landis

According to the book *Eight Men Out* by Eliot Asinof, gambling and organized baseball had an intriguing relationship going back to the game's origins. After a great start in 1877, the Louisville Grays lost seven straight games. Four players, accused of consorting with gamblers, were suspended from baseball for life by the Louisville club president. Responding to the charges, they claimed the Grays hadn't been paying them.

Stingy owners and reserve clause contracts made naïve and hungry players a logical target for gamblers. Gambling allegations came to a head late in the 1920 season when a Chicago grand jury began investigating reports that the Cubs had thrown a three-game series against the Phillies.

The probe expanded to include allegations against eight Chicago White Sox players and their poor performance in the 1919 World Series. Stars including "Shoeless" Joe Jackson, Eddie Cicotte, and Chick Gandil were accused of collaborating with known gangsters. Their heavily favored White Sox lost to the Cincinnati Reds, winning only three games in the best-of-nine Series.

Club owners were desperate to protect their investments, maintain control, and clean up baseball's image. The investigation dragged on into November 1920, when owners chose Major League Baseball's first commissioner and granted him virtually unlimited authority.

As a former federal judge, Kenesaw Mountain Landis feared no entity or individual. In 1907, he forced the powerful John D. Rockefeller to testify in the Standard Oil antitrust case. Landis fined the company over $29 million (although the decision was eventually overruled).

On July 28, 1921, all eight White Sox players were acquitted by a Chicago criminal court jury. Jurors may have been contemptuous toward the tight-fisted, unpopular White Sox owner Charles Comiskey. Despite their acquittal, before the verdict was even announced, Landis had banished the eight "Black Sox" players from organized baseball forever.

For the next quarter-century, Landis ruled the game with austerity. His legacy included creating a "gentleman's agreement" that prohibited major league teams from signing minority players.

It only took a few months for Landis to cross paths with an irreverent Babe Ruth.

A 1921 World Series Appearance

Some baseball historians claim the Bambino's 1921 season was his career best. In 540 at-bats, he had 204 hits, 171 RBIs, and batted .378. With 59 homers, he established a new big-league record for a third consecutive year.

Ruth propelled the Yankees to their first-ever World Series appearance. Playing a best-of-nine contest, the New York Giants triumphed in eight games. Ruth hit .313 with a homer.

Shortly after the Series, Ruth and teammate Bob Meusel scheduled a post-season barnstorming tour of the Northeast. The decision had severe and expensive consequences.

Not one to be trifled with, Landis had warned them against violating the 1914 World Series barnstorming prohibition. Nearly everyone thought the rule was pointless, but Ruth ignored both Landis and legal advice from Yankee ownership. Babe was more focused on an estimated $25,000 tour payoff (his 1921 regular season salary was $20,000). Hubris and greed trumped logic…and after all, he was Babe Ruth!

Ruth and Meusel played in Buffalo on October 16th, then four games in western New York and Pennsylvania. But, pressured by both a livid commissioner and nervous Yankee administrators, Ruth canceled the remaining tour.

The steely-eyed Landis came down hard. Ruth and Meusel had their $5,265 World Series bonus seized by the commissioner. And they were suspended for the first six weeks of the 1922 season; neither played until May 20th. Nearly everyone thought the penalty was too extreme for violating what appeared to be a ridiculous and arbitrary decree. That included President Warren Harding.

A Troubled 1922 Season

Despite the suspensions, Ruth and Meusel were permitted to attend spring training in New Orleans. Ruth played brilliantly in pre-season exhibition games as the Yankees worked their way north. He homered in Galveston, San Antonio, and Richmond.

Spring training included a March visit by Commissioner Landis in New Orleans. If the players were expecting leniency regarding their upcoming suspensions, they were disappointed. A photo from the day shows a scrawny, stiff-collared Landis in the center, seemingly gripping talons into the biceps of Ruth and Meusel. Landis could have been the archetype for Montgomery Burns from *The Simpsons*. You can imagine the thoughts behind the players' forced smiles.

Babe Ruth, Baseball Commissioner Kenesaw Mountain Landis, and Bob Meusel. The photo was taken when Landis met with the players at the Yankees Spring Training Camp in New Orleans, March 1922. The commissioner refused to reconsider his 33 game suspension of Ruth and Meusel to begin the upcoming regular season. It's not hard to imagine the thoughts behind the forced smiles.

Photo Credit: Wikimedia Commons

As the season got underway, watching games from the dugout was unbearable for Ruth. He finally took the field after missing thirty-three games. Babe struck out in his first at-bat, going hitless against the St. Louis Browns. The slump continued. His frustration boiled over when he was called out on a close play several days later. Throwing dirt at umpire George Hildebrand, Ruth was quickly ejected. Taunted as he left his hometown field, he jumped onto the Yankee dugout roof and challenged a boisterous heckler to a fight. The man fled. Luckily for Babe, he only received a one-game suspension.

Toning down his behavior, he played great baseball for several weeks. On June 6th in Chicago, he blasted a 480-foot home run and became the first hitter to clear Comiskey Park's center field fence.

But a clash with another umpire a week later led to a three-game suspension. Two more games were added when Ruth insisted on taking batting practice the day his suspension began. Yankee management responded by hiring private detectives to keep tabs on Ruth and his teammates for the remainder of the 1922 season.

Suspended for the first 33 regular season games by Commissioner Landis, Ruth watches Opening Day from the stands. The Yankees played the Washington Senators at Griffith Stadium on April 12, 1922.

Photo Credit: Wikimedia Commons

The following week, Ruth and Commissioner Landis met privately before a game in Boston. Landis promised to reconsider the World Series barnstorming ban later in the season. That assurance seemed to pacify Ruth and curbed further outbursts.

But due to the suspension Landis had imposed—and Ruth's mid-season misdeeds—Babe missed 42 games in 1922. He still finished his season with stats any player would envy: 35 HR, 96 RBI, and .315 BA. But Ruth and his many fans had higher expectations.

Edging the St. Louis Browns by a game, the Yankees again won the American League pennant. And once again, they faced the Giants in the 1922 World Series.

John McGraw's squad took the first game, 3-2. With Game 2 tied at 3-3 after ten innings, umpires ended the game due to impending darkness (major league baseball didn't add lighting until 1935). Officials ruled it a tie, and it wasn't completed. The Giants then swept the next three games to win the 1922 championship.

The Yankees' .287 regular season batting average tumbled to an anemic .203 in the Series. Ruth batted a microscopic .118 with only two hits, although several deep fly balls were hit directly to the Giants' outfielders. 1922 would be Babe's only World Series as a Yankee when he failed to hit a home run.

Visible across the East River from the Series, construction moved forward on a massive new stadium. The Giants owned the Polo Grounds but had been sharing it as an alternating home field with the Yankees since 1913. The Giants' pugnacious manager, John McGraw, had gotten fed up with the arrangement. What really irked him was seeing the Yankees draw larger crowds than his club.

No longer would the American Leaguers split home games with the Giants. They'd celebrate opening day in the Bronx on April 18, 1923, christening a colossal, three-tiered ballpark named Yankee Stadium.

1922 Barnstorming Arrangements

Two days after the 1922 World Series ended, Judge Landis finally rescinded the rule that had gotten Babe Ruth and Bob Meusel in hot water a year earlier. Babe had ambitious plans for a Great Plains barnstorming tour, figuring to earn $20,000 with sidekick Meusel netting $8,000.

The Big Fella was likely looking forward to escaping the Big Apple's harsh scrutiny. The *New York Tribune* reported, "It seems that someone had guaranteed them $1,000 per game to be played in Iowa, Nebraska, and points west…beyond the reach of the echoes from the recent strife at the Polo Grounds."

Columnist James Crusinberry wrote in the *New York Daily News*, "The Babe and the Bob can now go out and do their

stuff for the fans in the bush towns." Based on the published itinerary, Crusinberry had a valid point. Kansas City, Omaha, and Denver were included. But why was Sleepy Eye, Minnesota, chosen instead of the Twin Cities? Two stops in Oklahoma did not include Tulsa or Oklahoma City, but instead Bartlesville and Drumright.

According to "L.J. Galbreath of Kansas City, in charge of routing," the tour would kick off on October 13th and wrap up on Halloween in El Paso, Texas. Spread across ten states, *half the cities listed had populations of less than 25,000.*

How the barnstorming sites and dates were selected has been difficult to ascertain. But anticipating a pending Landis waiver, advance work had been underway for several weeks as the baseball season wound down. The Western Booking Agency coordinated logistics and contacted Midwestern ballparks about potentially hosting games.

The *Lincoln Star* reported in mid-September that the agency had called their city's minor league club. Skeptical, the Nebraska paper wrote, "The Kansas City gents are firm believers in the Barnum theory that 'a sucker is born every minute.' However, Babe and Bob will not do their act in Lincoln this fall—not at the rate of $2,000 per (game)."

They would be proven wrong.

The Knights of Columbus Connection

The Knights of Columbus played a role in barnstorming arrangements. In a 2019 article for the organization, Andrew Fowler highlighted the KC's involvement with Ruth and Meusel. Both had joined the Catholic men's fraternal group in New York.

Fowler wrote that in San Antonio on March 31st, 1922, the Yankees played an exhibition game against the Brooklyn Dodgers. Prior to the game, local Knights "… entered the grounds in mass formation before giving Ruth an engraved, sterling silver ball and bat." Ruth reciprocated by blasting a homer over the right-field fence, described as "…the longest hit…made in League Park."

Considering Babe was approaching a six-week suspension

to kick off his 1922 season, the adulation of the Knights of Columbus no doubt resonated with him. The Knights are mentioned several times as hosting Ruth and Meusel during their fall barnstorming tour.

Another group frequently mentioned as helping fund the tour is the American Legion. Local chapters of the newly formed organization hoped to raise money in several cities. Various civic leaders also bankrolled appearances.

Unfortunately, nearly everyone anticipating a big payoff would be disappointed.

The Influence of Christy Walsh?

A long-time press agent and spin doctor, Christy Walsh, created a newspaper syndicate in 1921. Specializing in profiling sports stars, he paid Babe Ruth and other famous athletes to "write insider stories" that appeared in papers around the country. In truth, the bylined columns were ghostwritten. But whether stories were fabricated or not didn't matter—the Christy Walsh Syndicate made newspaper publishers and famous athletes a pile of money.

Walsh pioneered modern celebrity boosterism, working tirelessly for his several dozen clients. His first signing was Ruth in early 1921. According to Jane Leavy in *The Big Fella*, by 1927, Walsh's financial acumen allowed Babe Ruth to become the first ballplayer to earn more money off the field

than on it. At that point, he "… now controlled every aspect of Ruth's financial life: investments, annuities, insurance policies, endorsements, personal appearances, and taxes. And he was involved in every aspect of Ruth's personal life, too." That included mitigating public criticism after his frequent violations of Prohibition-era "acceptable behavior."

Despite his evolving business relationship with Ruth in 1922, it doesn't appear that Christy Walsh helped coordinate the tour.

Babe's Fellow Barnstormer, Bob Meusel

Bob Meusel first broke in with the Yankees in 1920, the same spring Ruth joined the club. They shared outfield duties for nine seasons, alternating between positions. Whether Ruth or Meusel played left field or right depended on the ballpark and the sky; Ruth struggled more against bright sunlight.

An excellent ballplayer with Hall-of-Fame stats, Meusel spent ten years in New York and retired with a .309 batting average. In 1925, he led the American League with 33 homers (Ruth had several health issues that season). Meusel is also the only Yankee to hit for the cycle (a single, double, triple, and home run in the same game) three times.

Defensively, he is still ranked among the best outfield arms in baseball history. His older brother Emil (nicknamed

Brothers Emil "Irish" Meusel of the New York Giants and Bob Meusel of the New York Yankees. They faced one another in the World Series three times. This was taken on October 10, 1923.

Photo Credit: Wikimedia Commons

"Irish," although the Meusel family was French-German) played left field for the Giants. The Meusel brothers competed against one other in three consecutive World Series contests between 1921 and 1923.

Despite his immense talent, Meusel was criticized as "lazy and indifferent." Not always hustling on the diamond made him unpopular with teammates and fans. Quiet and aloof off the field, he didn't socialize with other players. But like Ruth, Meusel reportedly liked downing liquor and chasing skirts. Maybe that factored into their barnstorming relationship?

Bob Meusel, 1921.

Photo Credit: Wikimedia Commons

Spitballs, Merry Minstrels, and the Klan

Finally free on Wednesday to venture into the hinterlands (or fleece the yokels, depending on your viewpoint), the players left Grand Central Station on a westbound Pullman car.

The daily *Perry Chief* reassured their readers on Thursday, October 12th, that Ruth and Meusel "were in Chicago this afternoon and will arrive in plenty of time for the game." They quoted "E. E. Allison, manager of the national mid-west tour of the two big league stars," soon after his arrival from Kansas City.

The article included the Perry roster, chosen by Perry manager J. C. Collins. Ruth was slated to start in center field for the home team, "possibly switching to infield later" (he

Babe Ruth, front row right, and Bob Meusel, front row left, pose with a team from Perry, Iowa. Played on October 13, 1922, the game kicked off a seventeen-city tour.

Photo courtesy of Darcy Maulsby and Forest Park Museum, Perry, Iowa.

played first the entire game). The starting pitcher for Perry was Western League southpaw Joe Eddleman. That season with the Des Moines Boosters, Eddleman posted a 2-5 record in 11 games for the Class A team (equivalent to today's Triple A level).

On tour, Meusel generally played on the visiting team against Ruth. He'd be in center field for the Pella Meteors. "Windy" Zonderman and Paul Versteeg shared pitching duties. Perry and Pella had played one another earlier that summer, each winning a game.

Perry and central Iowa buzzed with anticipation. With good weather, promoters hoped to sell 4,000 tickets. The Des Moines & Central Iowa Railway—known locally as the

Inter-Urban—offered round-trip discounts from the capital city (interurban railways were generally short trolley routes between metro downtowns and outlying areas, powered by overhead electric lines).

Farmers took a break from husking corn and headed to town. Students lucky enough to have authentic (or forged) notes from their parents were dismissed early. Dime stores closed for the afternoon. A sports doubleheader would conclude that evening with high school football between Perry and arch-rival Jefferson.

Ruth and Meusel arrived at the Rock Island depot in Des Moines late Thursday afternoon. They were met by John

Bob Mesuel (seated on the left) and Babe Ruth pose with the Pella Meteors baseball team. Pella played against Perry on October 13, 1922. Seventh from the left in the back row is Paul Versteeg, who threw a spitball to strike out Ruth.

Photo courtesy of Pella Historical Society and Museums, Pella, Iowa.

McCarthy, who drove them forty miles to Perry. Local VIPs greeted the stars as young fans mobbed the smiling Babe. They spent the night at the Hotel Pattee.

Unfortunately, Friday's weather wasn't as warm and welcoming as the community had been. Intermittent morning showers and gusty winds kept away many travelers. Skies cleared after lunch.

Eddleman struggled early, walking Pella's first two batters. Heck Gale bunted to fill the bases. Batting clean-up, Meusel hit an inside curve to left-center "…with all his power sending it in the general direction of Medicine Hat." The local paper said Big Bob was "…turning the corner at third base when Peacock reached the ball, way out near the racetrack fence." *Des Moines Register* sports editor Sec Taylor wrote, "Bob just trotted around the bags and was sitting on the bench by the time the sphere had returned to civilization." The grand slam accounted for Pella's only runs. Meusel later singled and struck out twice.

Ruth tripled, driving in two runs in the bottom of the first. He struck out his next time up. Before the strikeout pitch, Taylor reported the Pella pitcher coughed on the ball "…before delivering in a way that is not considered good etiquette in the best of baseball circles." In short, Versteeg threw a spitball.

"Not to be outdone, 'the infant' tried to infringe on the rules himself by stepping up on the pitches eight or ten feet to catch them before they broke." Imagine pitching to Babe Ruth when he's only fifty feet away!

Babe's adjustment led to another triple. Meusel could have caught it "if he was in a hustling mood," wrote Taylor.

Babe hits a triple in Perry, Iowa.

Photo Credit: George Yates, Des Moines Register, 10/14/1922

Otherwise, for Meusel, "every move he makes is a picture." And Ruth "moved with unbelievable speed for a man built like a giant above the waist and just like a normal human being in the legs."

With 15 hits (and despite the spitballs), Perry crushed Pella, 12-4. Whirling dust contributed to several errors on both teams. The *Perry Chief* reported the stars were "...photographed, interviewed, toasted and made over, they shook hands with everyone, wrote their names on baseballs and score cards and left Perry last evening with the big end of the $1,055 gate receipts."

Due to the blustery weather, only 836 tickets were sold. The players were contracted to collect the first $2,000 of ticket sales.

Officers of the Perry American Legion had worked hard to finance the event, hoping to raise a little money. It must have been a bittersweet day for the men who had sacrificed so much—both in European trenches and from their wallets.

Action halted briefly during the game for an odd promotional stunt. The "Merry Minstrel Maids sent an advertising car of black beauties out to the ball grounds" to challenge the winning team. One cross-dressing man described as a "dusky damsel" posed in a photo with Babe, who "… seemed to enjoy it as much as she did," wrote the *Perry Chief.*

The interruption promoted two upcoming performances at the local Grand Theater. A double-column display ad for the Minstrel Maids promised "A Riot of Fun and Frolic in Black Face. Personally directed by Miss Lillian E. Hall. Admission 75c."

Underlying the racist shenanigans were more sinister elements. A 2017 *Perry News* article by historian Rod Stanley mentioned that the Ku Klux Klan had a large and active central Iowa presence in the early 1920s. Besides their infamous racial prejudice, the Klan was hostile toward Catholics and recent southern European immigrants. The group had recently rebranded itself as less hostile, soft-peddling itself as a civic-minded "Invisible Empire" dedicated to preserving white Protestant American values.

Well-known, unrobed KKK members attended the game, "…sitting in the stands that day with Catholics and cheered the Babe as if he were one of them."

A half-mile north of the fairgrounds, St. Patrick's Catholic Church dominated the skyline. Ruth had visited the church school before the game. It stood next to the lawn where the Klan had once burned a cross. The Catholic ballplayers joined their Knights of Columbus brothers for a banquet at the Hotel Pattee before leaving town.

Candy for the Kids in Lincoln

"BABY ISN'T CRYING," headlined a brief notice in the *Beatrice Daily Express* highlighting the Yankees' loss to the Giants, "Babe Ruth isn't crying about the world series (sic). He's barnstorming now with the Ruth-Meusel Dough Collecting Company. They'll be in Lincoln Saturday."

On a happier note, an October 13th ad in the *Lincoln Journal Star* promised "Good News for the Kiddies!" and informed their readers that the barnstormers would celebrate "National Candy Day" by handing out free Gillen & Boney candy bars at four children's charities in Lincoln. Saturday morning stops included the Tabitha Home, St. Thomas Orphanage, the Orthopedic Hospital, and the Home of the Friendless.

The *Lincoln State Journal* published two photos of the candy tour. One, at St. Thomas, features a long line–mostly boys in white shirts, puffy knickers, and dark ties—awaiting the players' arrival. An inset featured local candy mogul Frank Gillen flanked by two expressionless Yankees in suits, ties, and bright newsboy caps. The second picture shows several dozen elementary-age kids gathered in rows. A boy on his knees, dressed in coveralls and a short-sleeved shirt, reaches toward a towering Meusel for his candy bar. As usual, most eyes are focused on Babe. He's surrounded by a mix of boys and several curly-haired girls in baggy white dresses.

To celebrate National Candy Day, Babe and Bob distributed Gillen's Candies to over three hundred disadvantaged kids in several Lincoln institutions.

Photo Credit: *Lincoln Journal Star* (Lincoln, Nebraska), October 13, 1922

The players went inside to visit bedridden kids at the Orthopedic Hospital. "Ruth became greatly interested in the children here, particularly those in the baby ward…he wanted to hear about each case."

Bishop O'Reilly greeted the players at St. Thomas. Ruth and Meusel declined his lunch invitation, "as the players do not eat before they play." The players reportedly handed out 328 candy bars before heading to the ballpark.

Babe and Bob Take Turns Pitching

Landis Field had been built a year earlier by Buck Beltzer. Home field for the Lincoln Links (Nebraska State League, Class D), Beltzer named the stadium to honor baseball Commissioner Judge Landis. Did Ruth and Meusel appreciate the irony?

As the game progressed, Ruth struggled against southpaw Stewart "Red" Randall. He struck out swinging in the first. In the third, he hit three fouls before taking a called third strike. Turning to "Umpire Williams," Ruth "… tried to laugh that off with no success." He worked Randall to a full count his next time up, fouling off three more pitches before walking. Ruth was doubled-up off first after second baseman Carter caught a high pop-up.

Despite getting Ruth to ground out in the seventh, Randall gave up three runs. He finished his fine outing with eight strikeouts.

Going into the eighth inning, the barnstormers had combined for only one hit in seven at-bats. "They claimed the white sign which decorates the fence in line with the pitcher was to blame…but nobody was covering up the sign when Pug Griffin got his triple and double," said the *State Journal*. "Something had to be done and done quickly" to liven up the game.

The visiting Lawlor Sporting Goods team failed to score. Bob Meusel moved from first to pitch in the bottom of the eighth, holding Ruth and his Knights of Columbus team scoreless.

Not to be outdone, Ruth relieved pitcher Leo Smith in the top of the ninth. Leading off for Lawlor, Meusel cracked a home run to center. "That hit was worth half of the $643 the Yanks slipped into their pokes after the game," reported the *State Journal*. "Of course, there could have been no collusion between batter and pitcher."

Pitching again in the ninth, Meusel returned the favor. Ruth blasted a middle-of-the-plate fastball for a triple. According to the paper, those hits transformed a lackluster game into a finish "…as exciting as a circus chariot race."

Ruth and the Knights squeaked out a 7-6 win before a disappointing turnout of only 947 fans on a sunny afternoon. The Lincoln game wasn't even competing with Nebraska Cornhuskers football—they were off that Saturday.

The Lincoln Knights of Columbus hosted a banquet for the players following the game.

Two Dingers in Omaha

The tour continued Sunday in nearby Roarke Park, home of the Western League Omaha Buffaloes (Class A). Both Babe and Bob slammed homers for 4,000 lucky fans.

The *Omaha Daily Bee* reported Babe appeared at the ballpark "...dolled up in a brand-new Woodmen of the World ball uniform, which fit him like an army blouse fits a private." But the afternoon belonged to opposing Southside Merchants pitcher Art Dyck. He only gave up three runs, fanning 11 batters in seven innings.

The Merchants scored five in the first inning. Woodmen's starting pitcher, named Beers, walked the first two batters. Batting clean-up, Bob Meusel drove the second pitch over the right-field fence. The Merchants added two more runs after another walk, a double, and an error.

Dyck struck out Ruth, swinging, in the bottom of the first. Ruth reached on a fielder's choice in the fifth and was stranded after stealing second.

In the sixth, Meusel stunned fans by throwing out McKeague at home plate from left field with an "almost perfect" throw. According to the *Omaha Daily Bee*, catcher Wachtler barely had to move to snag the ball. Applauded as he left the field, Meusel "...took off his cap, bowed to the grandstand, and smiled" before entering the Merchants' dugout.

After playing first base, Babe pitched the final two innings. He struck out five, including Meusel.

The Bambino's final chance for fireworks came in the bottom of the ninth. Now pitching for the Merchants, Meusel threw Babe three consecutive balls. "The fans yelled for action, and immediately Mr. Meusel grooved one for his sidekick, who in turn knocked the ball over the St. Joseph hospital" for a two-run homer.

Despite the blast, the Merchants edged the WOW team, 7-5. The *Daily Bee* concluded, "...all in all, it was a big day for the fans."

Nebraska had witnessed two entertaining ballgames. The Cornhusker state would host a third game later that week, 455 miles west of Omaha.

Five Hundred Frigid
Baseball-Hungry Fans

After a boisterous crowd of thousands in Omaha, freezing rain the following afternoon limited attendance to about 500 hardy souls in Sleepy Eye, Minnesota. But two homers by Babe Ruth rewarded the chilly fans. And one of the retrieved home run balls made for a legendary story.

According to the September 27, 1922, edition of the *New Ulm Review*, games were scheduled for Minneapolis on October 15th and Sioux Falls two days later. Sleepy Eye—named to honor a local Sisseton Native American leader—lay halfway between the cities. Due to the "alertness of Sleepy Eye businessmen," the county seat town of 2,449 arranged to have a barnstorming game on the 16th. (It's undetermined

A postcard from Bob and Babe in Sleepy Eye, Minnesota, where they played on October 16, 1922.

Photo courtesy of Sleepy Eye Area Historical Society, Sleepy Eye, MN

why the Minneapolis game was canceled.) Promoters stated they could accommodate "a 10,000 crowd with any kind of favorable weather."

The *Mankato Free Press* wrote that Ruth and Meusel first arrived in Mankato, traveling overnight by rail nearly 300 miles from Omaha. According to the reporter, he was the only person on hand to greet the players and tour manager Al Allison. Nobody from Sleepy Eye—43 miles west—showed up for nearly 90 minutes.

The unnamed journalist described Bob Meusel as "a quiet sort of chap" and Babe Ruth as "…no gab fester himself… both seemed to want to discuss everything but baseball."

Allison was chattier. When told neither player would likely hit a ball over the Sleepy Eye fence, he responded that locals said the same thing in Perry, "…but Babe clouted one over the racetrack fence." (Allison was either mistaken or lying. Meusel hit a ball that rolled to the distant racetrack boundary, resulting in a grand slam. Ruth may have hit one that far while warming up, but not during the game). The road manager added that he hadn't encountered any problems with the temperamental Ruth during the tour.

The barnstormers eventually arrived in Sleepy Eye and checked into the Berg Hotel for some well-deserved rest. Promoters considered canceling the game due to sleet and arctic winds. "But when five hundred baseball-hungry fans stormed the gate with tickets, it was necessary to play the game regardless of weather conditions," wrote the *Free Press*. Meanwhile, "the main attractions were asleep in their hotel beds, certain the exhibition would not take place. When told that a large crowd was at the field, they gladly donned their uniforms and went to the ballpark." Ruth reportedly wore a pair of kid gloves to keep his hands warm.

Shivering but enthusiastic fans met the players at Sleepy Eye Athletic Park (the ballpark remains standing today and is still used). The Sleepy Eye band attempted to warm those arriving by "...playing some peppy selections" but were challenged by "...valves freezing with great frequency." The ball clubs were composed of "southern Minnesota all-stars"—some minor leaguers, semi-pro players, and Sleepy Eye natives.

The *New Ulm Review* wrote that Ruth homered in the first, scoring Davis. With the bases full in the fifth, he did it again. Babe "made two screaming home runs over center field, both being wicked liners and not rising more than fifty feet above the ground but clearing far beyond the ordinary center field territory." The *Herald-Dispatch* added that when Babe "...landed on the old apple, it cut through the frosty air at such a sizzling momentum that the surrounding atmosphere simply thawed, and the ball was wet with rain drops when it landed." Both were hit off Sleepy Eye's Sylvester "Sox" Schueller.

Ruth played second base, then pitched hitless ball in the final inning. Playing left field, Meusel failed to reach base. Babe's team won, 9-7, in six innings.

Additional seating had been built to accommodate a large crowd of up to 2,000 people. The local American Legion (and possibly the Knights of Columbus) helped underwrite the event. But the *Brown County Journal* reported that "...there was no guarantee of a minimum payment to the stars, so Babe and Bob gambled against the weather conditions, popularity, etc., and lost at Sleepy Eye."

St. Mary's High School in Sleepy Eye hosted a banquet afterward, sponsored by the Knights of Columbus. A dance followed at the Standard Opera House.

Two wonderful stories survive from that day.

"I'm Not Going to Run the Bases!"

An October 10, 2020, *Mankato Free Press* story commemorated the 98th anniversary of the Sleepy Eye game. It included portions of a 2012 interview posted on the Babe Ruth Central website. According to Ruth's daughter, Julia Ruth Stevens, her dad shared a story from that cold afternoon in Minnesota:

> *"Daddy and Bob each picked members of the town to be a part of their teams. Daddy picked this big, strapping man to join his team. Well, it doesn't sound like the gentleman had ever really played baseball before. But, when the guy went up to bat, he hit the ball so hard and so far that it went out into the woods well beyond the ballfield. Then he just stood there, so Daddy said,*

'Hey pal, what are you doing? You hit a home run— run the bases!' and the man replied, 'I'm not going to run the bases; I'm going to go and buy you a new ball!'"

Len Youngman, a Legendary Baseball, and a Photo Bomb

Leonard Youngman passed away in 2018 in Virginia, Minnesota, on the 96th anniversary of the Sleepy Eye game. He was 107.

While Babe was playing baseball, Len was playing with friends outside the ballpark. He heard a bat crack, and the crowd roared. "And here comes this baseball flying way over the centerfielder's head; he didn't even chase it. I picked it up and ran with it," he smiled during a TV interview.

It came off Babe Ruth's bat.

His grandson Joel Youngman inherited the prized baseball. In 2016, Joel contacted the Sleepy Eye Area Historical Society with his grandfather's story. Local baseball historians

Randy Krzmarick, Dean Brinkman, and Scott Surprenant drove five hours to the Iron Range city of Virginia to meet Len and Joel. The story aired on KARE 11-TV in Minneapolis, winning producer Blake Huppert a regional Emmy award.

"I can't imagine anyone coming this far, just for a damn baseball," Len Youngman joked when he met them. He said he forgot to ask Babe to autograph the ball.

A photo from that day is displayed at the Sleepy Eye Area Depot Museum. Bob Meusel wears a full-length overcoat with his hands in the pockets. Babe Ruth wears a white woolen Yankee sweater in dark trim, missing a button.

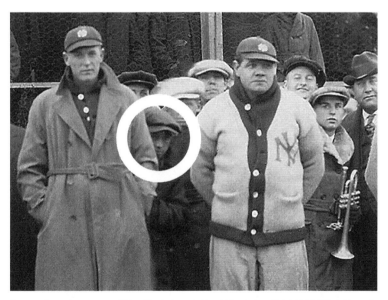

A precocious eleven-year old Len Youngman peeks at the camera from behind Bob Meusel's elbow. Len grabbed one of Babe's home run balls after it flew over the center field fence. He was featured on KARE TV in Minneapolis, with his grandson, in 2016. Len died at 107 on the 96th anniversary of the Sleepy Eye game.

Photo courtesy of Sleepy Eye Area Historical Society, Sleepy Eye, MN

Neither is smiling. They stand in front of a chicken-wire backstop, with about twenty men in the bleachers behind them. Eight other men huddle behind the players on the field.

Sneaking into the photo was a precocious lad sporting a newsboy cap. He peers out from behind Meusel's left elbow. Only his head is visible.

And as the shutter snapped, eleven-year-old Len Youngman photo bombed the Bronx Bombers.

A Parade, a New Glove for Babe, and a Blast from Meusel

After the game, the players and tour manager Allison were driven back to Mankato. They boarded an eight o'clock train for the four-hour trip to Sioux Falls.

The *Mankato Free Press* wrote: "It would be impossible to get a berth for the trip," so the party "…had to settle for three crowded seats in the smoker of the Northwestern." It was small consolation that Ruth could enjoy his cigars. He later complained about "rotten train service" during the trip, saying "the daily jumps did not agree with my sleeping hours." He had been unable to sleep on the overnight ride from Omaha to Mankato; this rail journey was no different. They checked into the Cataract Hotel after arriving in Sioux

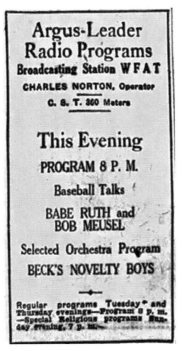

**Argus-Leader
Radio Programs**
Broadcasting Station W F A T
CHARLES NORTON, Operator
C. S. T. 360 Meters

___

This Evening

PROGRAM 8 P. M.

Baseball Talks

BABE RUTH and
BOB MEUSEL

Selected Orchestra Program

BECK'S NOVELTY BOYS

—◆—

Regular programs Tuesday and
Thursday evenings—Program 8 p. m.
—Special Religious programs Sun-
day evening, 7 p. m.—

WFAT Radio ad (Sioux Falls, SD) promoting
"Baseball Talks" with Babe and Bob.

Photo Credit: *Argus-Leader* (Sioux Falls, South
Dakota) · 17 Oct 1922

Falls around midnight.

The next morning, Babe left the hotel on a mission. Pleasantly surprised, he found exactly what he wanted at the Western Drug and Chemical Company store. "It was a great pleasure to be able to purchase a George Sisler model first base mitt in Sioux Falls," he told the *Daily Press*.

Sioux Falls mayor George Burnside had proclaimed Tuesday afternoon, October 17, 1922, to be "hours of recreation." Businesses and schools closed early.

Prior to the 2:30 p.m. game at East Side Park, Babe and Bob were honored with a Tuesday afternoon parade. Led by Captain Eric Elefson, some 500 American Legion members and a National Guard unit joined members of both baseball teams in the procession. The parade concluded at the ballpark.

A crowd estimated at between 1,300 and 1,500 fans endured frigid conditions under a bright blue sky. Meusel played right field for the Sioux Falls Congos, crowned that summer as local amateur league champions. Sporting his brand-new glove, Ruth anchored first base for the rival Kaysees team.

In the third inning, The Bambino blasted a grand slam over the right-field fence. The ball rolled all the way to an adjacent tennis court. Ruth added a single, double, and triple that afternoon—hitting for the cycle—and scored three runs.

Ruth also pitched three innings, giving up four hits. One was a two-run homer to Meusel. According to the *Daily Press*, Bob drove the curveball "...at least twenty feet over the scoreboard...some think it landed in the Sioux" [referring to the Big Sioux River].

The teams combined for eleven errors; cold weather was undoubtedly a factor. But in fairness to the players, baseball gloves were smaller and primitive compared to today. Fingers had yet to be laced together, the padding was thinner, and skimpy webbing between the thumb and index finger meant fielders were essentially catching balls with their palms. It was like trying to catch a baseball with a leather work glove. Bitter temperatures would have made this especially painful.

The Kaysees won, 10-7, in a two-hour game. Based on gate receipts, the local American Legion post pronounced the fundraiser "financially satisfactory."

That night, Babe gave a short speech on WFAT radio in Sioux Falls. Owned by the *Argus Leader* newspaper, it was one of only 30 radio stations on the air at the time. WFAT reached 15 states with a thin programming schedule. According to an *Argus* ad, the station aired "Regular programs Tuesday and Thursday evenings at 8 pm," with "Special Religious programs Sunday evening, 7 pm."

No wonder so few people owned radios in 1922.

"Very Ordinary Baseball" in Sioux City

Downriver from the quartzite rapids that gave Sioux Falls its name, the Big Sioux marks a ninety-mile boundary between Iowa and South Dakota. Flowing south, it joins the mighty Missouri River at Sioux City, the site of the next barnstorming game.

Boarding a Chicago, Milwaukee, and St. Paul train in Sioux Falls Wednesday morning, the barnstormers were greeted by Knights of Columbus members for their 10 a.m. arrival. A packed schedule awaited them.

Events kicked off with a "community motor tour." The players made brief appearances at several grade schools and visited St. Anthony's orphanage.

Shortly before noon, the trip concluded at the Sioux City

stockyards. "Hundreds of people cheered them from windows, roofs, and every point from which a view of the celebrities could be obtained," wrote the *Sioux City Journal*. A Lion's Club luncheon followed at the Martin Hotel, where both players spoke briefly.

Bob may have felt a bit slighted that morning. "About half the time, the official introducer even forgot the fact that the tall, rather bored-looking young man in the blue suit was Mr. Meusel."

Despite the pre-game hoopla, only about 700 attended the game at Mizzou Park that afternoon.

Ruth started at first and later pitched for the Stock Yards team. He had "two clean hits and one scratch hit; he walked once, struck out once, and was doubled off second base once." One of the four opposing pitchers was Lou Koupal, who later played for four major league teams.

Playing left field for Olson Sporting Goods, Meusel "chopped wind three out of five times …once with the bases full." He also singled and walked.

The local paper was unimpressed by the Yankee visitors. According to the *Journal*, Babe and Bob "played very ordinary baseball."

They lingered after the game to "monogram" baseballs for anyone who brought one.

An ad for the Sioux City game.

Photo Credit: *The Alton Democrat*
(Alton, Iowa), October 14, 1922

Seven Consecutive Foul Balls

The September 28th *Deadwood Pioneer-Times* announced that terms had been reached between the Western Booking Agency and the Deadwood Amusement Park. Babe Ruth and Bob Meusel would play ball in the Black Hills on Thursday, October 19th. Terms required a "…rain and snow insurance policy for five-hundred dollars payable to Ruth and Meusel, local auspices to pay the premium," in case of poor weather.

According to Google Maps, it's 459 miles—seven hours of freeway driving—between Sioux City, Iowa, and Deadwood, South Dakota. But I-90 didn't exist in 1922, nor was there direct rail service between the cities.

There are differing accounts of how the barnstormers made the western journey. The *Black Hills Weekly* reported the men were driven seventy-five miles to Norfolk, Nebraska, late Wednesday after their Sioux City game. In Norfolk, they boarded a Northwestern passenger train that had originated in Omaha.

Another story claimed the players left Sioux City right after the game, were driven straight to Omaha, and then boarded the train. Geographically and logistically, that doesn't make sense.

Either way, an overnight rail journey of well over 400 miles transported them to the Sturgis, South Dakota, depot at noon Thursday. They were greeted by a delegation from Deadwood. A short but twisting auto journey over "the new Boulder Park Road" delivered them to the host city for a luncheon.

To maximize attendance, schools and businesses closed early throughout the Black Hills region. Grandstand admission to Amusement Park was $1.10 (half price for kids), reserved seats were $1.65, and car parking was a dollar. Prices included a ten percent war tax. The ballclub also printed a "...most attractive score card booklet of 16 pages" selling "...at a very nominal charge" of ten cents.

The *Deadwood Pioneer Times* cautioned, "it is a great temptation for some to sneak thru the few broken places in the fence, but those who try will probably be the sufferer" due to an implied threat of heavy security.

Snow had been scraped from the ballfield a day earlier, but temperatures warmed, and the diamond was game ready. The Deadwood municipal band played Sousa marches as fans arrived. Many wondered if either Yankee would hit a ball over the center field fence. "It would be a distance fully equal

OFFICIAL SCORE CARD

"Babe" Ruth *and* "Bob" Meusel

home run hitters of the

NEW YORK AMERICAN

World Series Team

Playing With

DEADWOOD

and a picked team from the

BLACK HILLS LEAGUE

Thursday, Oct. 19th

At DEADWOOD, SO. DAK.

Game Called at 2 O'clock

PRICE TEN CENTS

The front page of a program sold in Deadwood, South Dakota. They played there on October 19, 1922.

to Ruth's longest drive," according to the *Sioux Falls Argus-Leader*. A paid crowd of 954 enjoyed balmy weather for the 2 p.m. contest.

Ruth played for Deadwood, recent Black Hills League champions. Meusel joined an all-star squad from other league clubs. Sturgis, Lead, Rapid City, Spearfish, and Aladdin (Wyoming) each supplied two players.

Babe excited fans by smashing several long balls during batting practice. But during the game, he doubled, walked, and struck out twice. He whiffed on three pitches from Chester Meade, "…although Babe tried hard to kill the ball and the strike out was no fluke," according to the *Lead Daily Call*.

He gripped his 48-ounce bat, anxious for a big hit in the bottom of the seventh. Working the count to 3 and 1, Babe then slammed seven consecutive fouls. "Some of them (went) over the grandstand, some of them into the grandstand, and some of them out over the line of cars, but none over the outfield fence or even close to it." Babe finally blooped a single for his second hit.

Deadwood beat the Black Hills League All-Stars 4-2. Meusel was hitless, popping out three times and striking out.

One local paper appreciated the Yankee efforts: "… they certainly tried hard to live up to the reputations that preceded them." The *Deadwood Pioneer Press* was less gracious. Their writer saw no reason for New Yorkers to wait hours "…to secure a ticket permitting them to see these fellows perform."

The Gaiety Orchestra played to a huge crowd that night at the Deadwood Auditorium. Ruth and Meusel skipped the festivities and boarded a southbound sleeper car for a 150-mile trip to Chadron, Nebraska.

"A Couple Little Bingles" in Scottsbluff

Greeting Babe and Bob the next morning in Chadron was C. N. Minner, who owned a local Essex-Hudson car dealership. Minner shuttled them a hundred miles across the desolate Nebraska panhandle to Scottsbluff for their Friday afternoon game.

The unique twin geological monoliths named Scotts Bluff and Chimney Rock tower over the North Platte River. Seen from miles away, they were vital landmarks to countless western migrants along the Oregon Trail. The city named Scottsbluff, founded in 1899 by a Burlington Railroad subsidiary, was established nearby.

The October 13th issue of the *Scottsbluff Star-Herald* announced that teams would be split between players living

Car dealer C N Minner from Scottsbluff transported the players from Chadron to Scottsbluff to Kimball, NE. A trip totaling nearly 300 miles.

Photo Credit: *The Farmers Exchange*
(Bayard, Nebraska), December 14, 1922

east and west of the Platte. Hometowns ranged over a 70-mile stretch between Bridgeport, Nebraska, and Yoder, Wyoming. "The valley, while of course containing no particular Cobbs, nor Ruths nor Meusels nor Sislers, yet has an abundance of really good baseball talent, and this will be thoroughly combed and two excellent teams secured," claimed the paper.

Slack-jawed fans saw Babe hit several warm-up pitches out of the park and onto a nearby street. Anticipating similar action during the game, a dejected crowd instead watched him go hitless in four at-bats, striking out twice.

"Ruth went without a run of any kind, whiffing a couple of times and being tossed out at first on a couple of little bingles…the crowd got a good deal of fun razzing Babe," according to the *Farmer's Exchange*.

Meusel was three for four, slamming a center-field homer in his final at-bat. A local slugger named Purcell allegedly blasted a round-tripper that went equally as far.

The *Exchange* concluded that neither Ruth nor Meusel "…looked much better than the semi-professional company they were playing with."

Reports vary, but only between 300 and 500 people attended the game. The players remained overnight in Scottsbluff, home to 7,000 western Nebraskans. After several rumbling overnight train rides, they probably appreciated sleeping in a bed that wasn't moving.

Eastward to the Home of an Octagonal Mule Barn

For the miles that lay ahead to reach their next game, it was a very early wake-up call.

Saturday morning, C. N. Minner once again met the players, driving them 45 miles to Kimball, Nebraska. After boarding an eastbound Union Pacific, they chugged 470 miles through Ogallala, North Platte, and Kearney, past expansive cattle ranches, stubbled wheat fields, and rolling sand hills. Shortly after crossing the Big Muddy, they finally reached Tarkio, Missouri.

Tucked into far northwestern Missouri, Tarkio was famous for two things: an octagonal Mule Barn and a Presbyterian liberal arts college. About 3,000 people lived in the agricultural community.

Pitching for the home team, Tarkio native Frank Withrow had been a Phillies catcher for several years. He faced a lineup from nearby Hamburg, Iowa. Another major league veteran, "Brown, formerly of the Brooklyn team," started for the visitors. According to the *St. Joseph News-Press*, a capacity crowd filled the recently expanded bleachers.

Tarkio cruised to an easy 18-4 victory. But Babe Ruth contributed little to the effort, with only a single and a double. He also slammed a deep fly to Meusel late in the game.

"BABE FAILS TO DELIVER," headlined the *St. Joseph News-Press*. The subhead read, "Home-Run King Is Not Up to Specifications in Tarkio Game—Meusel Also a Bust."

The guys may have been a little tired. After boarding a train eleven days earlier, and a few short days after losing the World Series—Ruth and Meusel had traveled 1,200 miles from New York to Perry, Iowa. Since then, they had endured 2,300 miles of small-town train trips and bumpy car rides before reaching Missouri. That included a 515-mile journey the morning of the Tarkio game. Babe and Bob had played nine games in nine days in five states, battling sleet, dust devils, and spitballs.

At least their next stop was a short hundred miles away. Organizers planned a Sunday afternoon doubleheader in Kansas City. The marquee game pitted the New Yorkers against several Negro Leaguers who would one day be inducted into the Baseball Hall of Fame.

Quality Baseball in K.C., 1922

Although lacking a major league club until the Philadelphia Athletics relocated in 1954, Kansas City had a rich baseball tradition. In the early 1920s, the area hosted two outstanding teams. Both played at Association Park, located a few blocks away from the present-day Negro League Museum in downtown Kansas City.

The American Association, double-A Kansas City Blues finished 1922 with a 92-76 record. The all-white team also drew a league-high 307,000 fans. A year later, they went 112-54. The 1923 Blues are still ranked among the top 100 all-time minor league teams.

The Kansas City Monarchs played in the Negro National League; an organization formed several years earlier by Rube

Foster. In 1922, the eight-team league also included the Indianapolis ABCs, Chicago American Giants, Cleveland Tate Stars, Detroit Stars, Pittsburgh Keystones, St. Louis Stars, and the Cuban Stars West (based in Cincinnati).

Pitcher "Bullet" Joe Rogan not only compiled a 15-8 record for the Monarchs but also batted clean-up and hit .368 with 15 homers. Other stars included third baseman Dobie Moore, hitting .380, and pitcher Rube Currie who was 12-7.

The Monarchs became a celebrated Negro League franchise for over 40 years. Fourteen former players are in the Baseball Hall of Fame, including Rogan and teammate Jose Mendez. Among future Monarch legends were Jackie Robinson, Satchel Paige, and Ernie Banks.

The Monarchs posted a 47-31-2 record in 1922. In early October, they faced the Blues to determine who had the best metro team. Promoters planned a best-of-nine series at Association Park. But in just six games, the Monarchs were crowned "The New City Champions of Kansas City." The series win gave Black ballplayers national recognition for the first time.

American Association Commissioner Thomas Hickey was outraged and embarrassed. He immediately prohibited his all-white league from scheduling any future games against Black players.

That didn't matter to "Babe Ruth's All-Stars." The Bambino and Meusel welcomed a challenge from the best team in Kansas City.

A Cold and Rainy Afternoon
Against the Monarchs

"In a big gas wagon," Babe and Bob arrived at soggy Association Park ten minutes before game time, both sporting raincoats over their Yankees' road uniforms. Despite chilly and misty conditions, about 2,000 fans showed up. That didn't generate a profit, wrote the *Kansas City Kansan*, since "Ruth and Meusel were guaranteed 1,000 berries each."

Ruth blasted four balls out of the park during batting practice. One allegedly cleared two houses beyond the right-field fence.

But during the game, the *Times* reported, "…there was a spot in right field that Babe picked out and at each appearance …he drove a single." Rube Currie tried to fool him with a slow ball, but Ruth "shot it to right like a shot."

If the Bambino couldn't flex his power, he'd show the Monarchs he could still pitch. Right fielder Ruth swapped positions with starting pitcher Quinn in the seventh. According to the *Kansas City Times*, Quinn "...mussed things up in general...misjudged three easy flies, let a ground ball single roll through his legs...before Babe could get them out, the Monarchs had cinched the game. With any kind of support, Ruth would have retired the side scoreless."

Bob Meusel, with a "pegging arm of steel," impressed fans with an accurate throw from deep center that almost nailed a runner at home. He singled twice, striking out in the sixth against Currie. It "made the big negro pitcher smile all over."

Soggy balls contributed to a sloppy game. Ruth's All Stars had six errors; each team had a wild pitch and a passed ball. After eight rain-shortened innings, the Monarchs claimed a 10-5 victory. Heavy Johnson hit a right-field homer for the victors.

A second game between two different clubs was rained out after two innings. Ruth singled for the Prince Howard's Orients, who beat the William R. Nelson American Legion squad 9-1. Meusel doubled for Nelson.

For the sixth time in seven games, the Negro League Kansas City Monarchs had beaten a white ball club. Dominance by black teams was common, according to Ken Burns' *Baseball* documentary. "Over the years, black baseball stars played their white rivals at least 438 times in off-season exhibition games...blacks won 309." That's a 70.5% winning percentage.

By scheduling the Monarchs, Babe Ruth thumbed his nose at Thomas Hickey and the Klan and any other racists in the old "Bloody Kansas" territory. He loved playing baseball, embracing competition against players or teams irrespective of skin color. That made him extremely popular with black fans. They—along with other exploited "little

Jose Mendez, a future Hall of Famer for the Kansas City Monarchs, played against Ruth on a rainy Sunday afternoon.

Photo Credit: Wikimedia Commons

people"—embraced Ruth. His background paralleled their own; he gave them hope that just maybe the American Dream could happen for them, too.

And he had no problem telling authorities to get screwed.

A Late Arrival to Leavenworth

Rain in the Kansas City metro area affected travel arrangements the next day.

Today, suburban Leavenworth, Kansas, is a half-hour drive from downtown KC. Driving took much longer a century ago, even in good weather. But after heavy rain, roads became greasy quagmires.

To visualize what travel in the 1920s may have been like, take a two-lane highway outside a city like Des Moines after a big rain. Turn onto a gravel road along a river valley. You may eventually encounter a "Level B" road sign. It receives minimal maintenance from the county. Even with a four-wheel-drive pickup, you might think twice about venturing further.

Now imagine driving a twenty-horsepower Model T down that road with wheels the same width as modern 'fat tire' bikes but with smoother tread. That's what rural travel could be like before Route 66 and the Lincoln Highway.

Despite heavy rains, Ruth and Meusel had planned to arrive at noon via "motor car" to Leavenworth. Due to the impassible roads, they opted instead for the interurban. Arriving too late to catch the 11 o'clock train, they had to wait three hours before leaving Kansas City.

Ruth bounded from the interurban rail car "…nattily attired in a dark suit…the picture of health. Meusel too was looking fine." At the park, both players agreed that hitting a ball over the deep right-field fence would be challenging.

Leavenworth was a military outpost dating back to 1827 before becoming a key supply base for western pioneers. In 1885, the Leavenworth Soldier's Home opened to benefit disabled and aging Civil War veterans.

On Monday, October 23rd, Babe joined a Soldier's Home baseball team stocked with several other major leaguers. The Leavenworth roster included starting pitcher Bill Burwell, a local who had recently been a reliever for the St. Louis Browns. His battery mate was Pat Collins, also from the area. Collins eventually had a ten-year big-league career, joining Ruth and Meusel as a New York Yankee in 1926.

Rival club Bonner Springs featured their own stars. Pitching for them was Claude Hendrix, who had recently retired from the Cubs with a 144-116 career record. He won 29 games in 1914 for Chicago's Federal League team. His catcher was Mac Wheat, "formerly of the Brooklyn Nationals."

Both Ruth and Meusel knew several of the players. Long Bob even recognized a former rival from his Pacific Coast League days, Ollie Kirmeyer.

The *Leavenworth Times* reported that new seating had been built in anticipation of a huge turnout. An estimated 2,000 fans could be accommodated; promoters hoped for as many as 3,000. Lennie Rafter, business manager for the Soldier's Home, quipped, "...there's plenty of room on the grass for those unable to obtain seating room."

The field had been soggy from Sunday's rain. "Much work was required to get the field into shape. The infield was raked and then burned with gasoline," said the paper.

Ruth doubled in the first. He later singled, walked, and flew out to Meusel. Meusel provided the firepower for Bonner Springs. In the third, he "...parked the ball over the left-field fence in one of the longest hits ever seen on the field," according to the *Leavenworth Post*. Another blast appeared to be leaving the park in the eighth. But Meusel's old friend Kirmeyer reached above the fence for a one-handed grab to rob him of a second homer. He struck out against Burwell twice.

During the game, guards kept busy trying to corral young fans from mobbing the players—especially Babe. The Bambino autographed "...schoolbooks, cards, tablet paper, and even the back of pieces torn from cracker jack boxes," said the *Post*.

Leavenworth won, 4-3. The *Times* reported that 1,200 fans watched the game.

Afterward, the players greeted several hundred fans at

Leavenworth's National Hotel. Neither commented on rumors that they may be traded in the coming weeks. Both also deflected questions about Yankee manager Miller Huggins and his alleged unpopularity with his players. Puffing a cigar, Ruth said he wished he could play at Sportsman's Park in St. Louis more often, where "…the right-field fence was very short" and much to his liking.

Ruth regretted that their late arrival had prevented a visit to St. Vincent's Orphanage. He autographed six baseballs for the charity's upcoming fundraiser, then the players headed back to Kansas City to spend the night.

"Boob" Ruth in Bartlesville

Bartlesville hosted the barnstormers the following day. Two hundred miles southwest of Kansas City, it lay just south of Kansas in the 15-year-old state of Oklahoma. The oil boomtown of 14,417 was the corporate headquarters for Phillips 66, founded five years earlier with 27 employees.

On September 22, a local paper wrote that the Bartlesville-based Empire Gas and Fuel Company had been in contact with tour managers. They were apparently willing to finance arrangements "if they do not hold out for too much money."

The Sunday before the game, the *Bartlesville Enterprise* reported that local pitchers "Meeks and Humphries are both in the peak of condition." To determine who would pitch against Ruth, they agreed to run a one-hundred-yard dash prior to the game.

Several players from the nearby Coffeyville (Kansas) Refiners had been recruited to play. One local paper even claimed that Coffeyville native Walter Johnson would "probably" pitch (fake news). The Washington Senators' legend faced Ruth and Meusel often enough during the regular season and probably didn't want to see them in a red dirt exhibition.

Neither Yankee impressed the Okies. According to "an eyewitness" writing for the *Enterprise*, "Babe is mud clear up to his neck, and Meusel's shins are pretty well gummed up with Mother Earth." Ruth was "positively punk," according to another report. The *Nowata Daily Star* even called him "Boob" Ruth!

Fans left early; half were gone by the seventh inning—those who remained finally got to see some unpredicted action.

A fistfight had broken out between two schoolboys near the rightfield bleachers. Kids egged them on, and even "…Babe left the perch on first and started rooting." Soon all the players were watching, with some placing bets on the outcome. "Just when things were really getting good, one of the boys was recognized by his mother—well, you know the procedure in such cases…" reported the *Enterprise*.

Things settled down, and play resumed. Ruth struck out to end the game. But to pacify the crowd, he took a few more swings before blasting a pitch into the left-field bleachers. Meusel's team won, 10-5.

Babe attended a Knights of Columbus dance later, where "he led the grand march."

A Dick Named Kelly

Later that week, the *Bartlesville Enterprise* published separate interviews with the barnstormers. Ruth told about a guy named "Kelly" they had met earlier during the season. Kelly had ingratiated himself with the players, buying beers and betting alongside them at the horse track. Jimmy Kelly was actually an undercover detective hired by Commissioner Landis to document off-field Yankee misdeeds.

According to writer Jane Leavy in *The Big Fella*, Landis and Yankee management employed Kelly after Ruth's five-day June suspension in Cleveland. Ruth had kicked dirt and cursed at umpire Bill Dinneen after charging in from left field.

Although Prohibition was in effect, "...Kelly wasn't above

a little entrapment," wrote Leavy. "He plied the players with so much booze in St. Louis that they begged him to join them in Chicago, where he arranged a trip to a Joliet brewery and suggested a group photo be taken, copies of which he got each of the duped revelers to sign."

Several bartenders tipped Ruth off to Kelly's real identity. Pitcher Carl Mays refused to believe it, saying, "Kelly was too much of a good fellow to be a detective." But Ruth said one day, "Kelly disappeared and shortly after the storm broke."

Kelly's photos landed on the Commissioner's desk. Landis met the Yankees in Boston "...to deliver some fire and brimstone, along with additional fines." This may have been the same meeting when Landis said he would reconsider his post-World Series barnstorming ban. Leavy noted that the Yankees retained the Burns Detective Agency for the remainder of the season.

Ruth called Kelly a "dick," saying if the players ever ran across him again, "...the Irish confetti is going to be showered upon him." (He was referring to a contemporary term for rocks thrown by immigrants during New York City riots.)

Meusel concurred. Addressing rumors that the Yankees were bribed to play poorly in the post-season, "...the talk that any of us laid down in the series is false," he concluded.

Ruth had been suspended four times in 1922, totaling 44 days (including the Landis barnstorming suspension). According to Yankee team ledgers, he'd been fined $10,719.95 of his $52,000 salary.

"A Loafing Game" in Drumright

After Bartlesville, Ruth and Meusel stayed at the Hotel Tulsa, halfway to their next destination. Eating breakfast in bed the next morning, Ruth told a reporter that the Yankees hoped to play in their city the following spring.

Another Oklahoma boomtown, Drumright, lay forty miles west of Tulsa. The town sprung up nearly overnight in 1912 when a wildcatter struck oil on a nearby farm. Oil workers, merchants, and gamblers overwhelmed the city quicker than housing could be built. By 1920, the census reported a population of 6,460 (losing nearly 1,500 residents in the coming decade). Inexplicably, Drumright hosted the next barnstorming contest.

Prior to the game, a Republican candidate for Oklahoma

governor shook hands with Ruth. Babe confessed to politi-
cian John Fields that he had "…a hell of a cold," and the trip
was "…pretty good, but there's so much jumping around."
The PR stunt didn't help Fields; he only got 44% of the vote
a few weeks later.

The star players again failed to impress an Okie crowd.
Taking the field in the first, Ruth smiled and "doffed his little
hat" to a roaring crowd, according to the *Drumright Weekly
Derrick*. But in the third, "Babe Ruth, king of the swinging
bat, struck out" with the bases full. Later he struck out again
and committed an error. As the game progressed, "…the
crowd was sure we had a good many players who could stay
on speaking terms with a ball better than either Babe or Bob."

Playing for Drumright, Long Bob homered and tripled
but also had three errors. With Bob pitching late in the game,
Ruth doubled off Meusel for his only hit.

The *Muskogee Times-Democrat* wrote that the New
Yorkers had played a "loafing game." Visiting Shamrock beat
Drumright, 7-5, before about a thousand fans.

Babe Ruth shared the Shamrock roster with another major
leaguer. Starting pitcher Moses Yellow Horse had played for
the 1922 Pittsburgh Pirates. Born in Indian Territory on a
Pawnee reservation that soon became the state of Oklahoma,
Yellow Horse was the first full-blooded Native American to
play major league baseball. Used primarily as a reliever, he
compiled a respectable 8-4 record in two years with the
Pirates. Sadly, his brief career succumbed to the twin demons
of injury and alcohol.

Fireworks in Fort Scott

If a single barnstorming game met everyone's expectations, it happened in sunny Fort Scott, Kansas, on October
26th. Hugging the Missouri border a hundred miles south of
Kansas City, the former military town buzzed with excitement.

The *Fort Scott Daily Tribune* wrote that Ruth and Meusel,
"…accompanied by their booking managers, Galbreath and
Conley, will arrive in Fort Scott on a noon Frisco train."
Eager fans arrived from up to 75 miles away.

Batting clean-up in the first for Fort Scott, Ruth homered.
The paper noted, "…it was not a clean-cut one, although it
allowed the great Bambino to circle the bases. The ball went
a mile high, and outfielder Jackson misjudged it badly." Babe
also tripled, singled, and "…played a great game at first base."

Bain, relieving for the visitors from Nevada, Missouri, struck out Ruth in the seventh. "This feat caused him to smile and no doubt upset his nerves as the Fort Scott batters came back in the eighth and pounded him for five runs."

Ruth took the mound in the sixth inning for Fort Scott, taking over for "China" Brown after he surrendered eight runs. Babe pitched brilliantly, striking out eight batters in three innings. Facing Meusel in the eighth, "...the Babe put one over the heart of the plate and Meusel hit it a mile to right field...it looked like an act of brotherly love on Ruth's part."

The paper didn't seem impressed with the fielding abilities of "sideshow attraction" Long Bob. Playing first base instead of his usual spot in left field, "...twice local batters hit ground balls off his shins."

Nevada shortstop Glenn Wright, who hit .299 that season with the Kansas City Blues, had three hits. Wright later spent eleven years in the majors with Brooklyn and Pittsburgh. Against the Cardinals on May 7, 1925, he became one of only fifteen players in major league history to record an unassisted triple play.

Fort Scott won the game, 11-9.

A contented Ruth said, "The players here were more agreeable than in other towns where we had played." Babe and Bob each pocketed $652.

While in Fort Scott, Ruth placed a $24 phone call (equal to $360 today) to his wife Helen in New York. A week earlier, Mrs. Ruth had suffered slight injuries when "...her husband's racer skidded into a tree on Pelham Parkway" in New York. The car sustained $900 in damages ($13,500 today). In comparison, a 1920 Model T retailed for $300.

The Daily Tribune later reported that five travelers from Chanute, Kansas, didn't reach the game until the fourth inning. During their trip to Fort Scott, their car tires had "four punctures." Hopefully, they had better luck driving 55 miles home in the dark!

A Pitcher's Duel in Pratt, Until it Wasn't!

Leaving Fort Scott, the tour steamed 230 miles west to Pratt, Kansas, halfway between Wichita and Dodge City.

The *Pratt Daily Tribune* urged folks to buy tickets in advance. Grandstand admission was $1.10, including the dime war tax. Car parking was $1.00; rumors circulated that rates as high as $5.00 might be charged on game day.

The *St. John Weekly News* reported that "…the players, their manager, and a woman *(probably neither Mrs. Ruth or Mrs. Meusel)* arrived by local passenger" at St. John, Kansas. The italicized words were part of the story, leading readers to speculate on her identity. A scandal brewing on the Kansas prairie?

The four individuals hopped into a car for a thirty-mile

ride from St. John to Pratt.

The Pratt paper had colorful observations about Bob Meusel prior to the game. Described as Ruth's "temperamental teammate" and "...a holy terror with the stick when he gets started," he had "...great accuracy in whipping the pellet, and his eccentric ways of hitting or being in a slump are well known."

On a warm and gusty Friday afternoon, an excited 1,800 fans filled the Rock Island Park grandstand in Pratt (population 5,200). Later, the Pratt High School football team would tangle with archrival Kingman.

Eldon Shupe started for the Pratt Legion team. He had pitched minor league ball for Joplin, Grand Island, and Denver, and had plans to join Omaha in 1923. In the meantime, he coached varsity football for Pratt.

The visitors hailed from Belpre, Kansas. They featured "Chief Boles, an Indian," who pitched earlier that season with the White Sox. He had faced six batters in his only major league game.

Shupe had beaten Boles a year earlier, shutting out Belpre, 1-0. The crowd wondered how Ruth and Meusel would fare against their local aces.

Unlike the 13 runs scored in six innings a day earlier, the first six innings in Pratt featured—as expected—great pitching. Pratt scored once in the first on two hits and a sacrifice. In the second, Meusel singled for Belpre and eventually scored. Belpre notched a second run in the fourth. Then Foster homered for Pratt, tying the score at 2-2 after six innings.

Everything changed in the seventh when coach Eldon

Shupe left the mound to prep his high school football team.

Fans yelled for Ruth to pitch, and Pratt manager Joe Foster obliged. Many had heard about Babe striking out eight in Fort Scott the day before. Some hoped the pitching duel would continue. Babe decided to throw batting practice instead, spiting the hometown crowd.

According to the *Pratt Daily Tribune*, the crowd was "…sorely disappointed when the king of swat deliberately wavered and laid down on the job. The visiting team hit his offerings at will and ran up a 13-2 score in the remaining three innings."

Compliments of Ruth, Meusel homered twice for Belpre.

The *Wichita Daily Eagle* wrote, "…the Belpre players almost ran over each other around the diamond. Ruth resembled a has-been very much. He was out solely for the money but would not get the price of a cigar, should he ever attempt another barnstorming trip through Kansas." Umpire Harry Allphin told the paper, "…he wants to forget that incident in his life as soon as possible."

Eighteen hundred fans saw the baseball game. Three thousand watched Eldon Shupe and his Pratt footballers beat Kingman, 12-6.

Teaming up in Pueblo with Speedy, Dunk, and Hook-Ball

Pueblo, Colorado, lies 350 miles west of Pratt, Kansas.

The barnstormers got a 50-mile head start toward their next exhibition after playing in Pratt, according to a note in the *Kinsley Graphic.* "Babe Ruth, Bob Meusel, Manager and wife spent Friday evening in Kinsley, leaving for the west on No. 5."

So—*the mystery woman was the road manager's wife?* Scandal averted!

In a final marathon small-town trip, Santa Fe's "No. 5" chugged and clanged past endless rippling seas of bluestem, brome, and switchgrass. The high plains gradually gave way to foothills and the Rocky Mountain Front Range city of

Pueblo.

The region had been devastated by a flash flood a year earlier. Heavy rain in the Arkansas River basin sent a cascade down the foothills and through Pueblo's downtown. Hundreds drowned in the deluge; hundreds more went missing. Some bodies were never recovered. Damage estimates reached into the millions as buildings, livestock, and livelihoods were all swept downstream.

Ten feet of water covered Merchants Park in June 1921. By October 28, 1922, the ball field had been restored, prepped, and was game-ready for the visiting major leaguers.

Rival city newspapers sponsored the two teams. Ruth played for the *Pueblo Chieftain*; Meusel for the crosstown

Babe posing with the victorious Chieftain Indians team in Pueblo. Back, L to R: Dauss (Doss) Barger, Harry "Speedy" Kilfoy, Allen Mays, George "Babe" Ruth, Dick Price, Frank Dunda. Bottom, L to R: Steve "Dunk" Sabo, Herb Kendall, Bill "Hook-ball" O'Conner, Bernie Jacklovich, Happy Kasel, Nick Badovinac. The two bat boys are thought to be newsboys for the Pueblo Chieftain newspaper.

Photo courtesy of the Pueblo County Historical Society, Pueblo, CO

Star-Journal. Despite being backed by two publications, game coverage is hard to uncover. However, a Pueblo County Historical Society photo features Babe with the "victorious Chieftain Indians." The caption identifies his teammates, including "Speedy" Kilfoy, "Dunk" Sabo, and "Hook-Ball" O'Connor. A sober Ruth stands in the back row, his hands on his hips and looking road-weary but resigned to playing yet another game.

Ruth and Meusel arrived in Denver five hours later than scheduled for their final game the next day. Weather didn't seem to be a factor.

Had they gotten to the Mile High City as originally planned, they were slated to headline an American Legion fundraiser. Following dinner, they would have enjoyed the live production "Slippery Gulch," publicized in advance as a *"naughty show."*

But it's easy to imagine the hard-drinking Yankee teammates not feeling guilty about ghosting yet another rubber-chicken 'guest-of-honor' dinner in the hinterlands. Hadn't there been one (or more) at every stop? And on a Saturday night, the eve of their final exhibition, and banged up after playing in seventeen ballgames in eight states, they may have spent some extra time out of the spotlight in Pueblo to celebrate the conclusion of a grueling tour with their own *naughty show*.

If that's what happened that night, they certainly figured they had earned it.

A Big Finale for Babe in Denver

A fine golfer with a five handicap, Babe Ruth once hit a 220-yard hole-in-one at a Long Island country club. But the whirlwind tour hadn't allowed any time for Babe to hit the links.

The Bambino swung a golf club "…with the same follow thru in baseball that is regarded as desirable in golf," reported the *Fort Collins Express*. They added that Ruth would be showcasing his driving skills before the game in Denver.

Colorado state golf champion Dr. Lawrence Broomfield reputedly drove golf balls farther than anyone in the Rockies. The *Express* reported that Broomfield and Ruth would challenge one another to see who had the longest tee shot. Doc Broomfield would go first, hitting a drive "…from some point in center field." Then, "Babe will wallop a ball from the same spot toward the stands." The story didn't indicate whether this was to happen *before* or *after* fans were seated (or whether helmets would be provided). If the contest occurred, no results were reported.

To push ticket sales, the *Denver Times* speculated that baseball barnstorming "...may be taboo after this year" and falsely claimed both players arrived "with sixteen homers each." The Yankees would face one another on hand-picked, local all-star teams. Ruth played first base for manager "Milliken;" Meusel joined a club managed by a man named "La Salle."

Profits were to benefit the local American Legion. The *Times* described the group and their fundraising goal as "...young patriots who have in mind the erection of a building in this city to preserve memories of their glorious feats in battle for Uncle Sam." Congress had chartered the American Legion in 1919 after the first World War.

Blustery snow flurries limited the Denver turnout. But perhaps enticed by the altitude and grateful the tour was finally ending, Ruth gave a chilly crowd their money's worth. He blasted two homers into the mile-high air, along with a double.

The *Butte Miner* reported in early November that former local boy Bill McKenzie had pitched in the game, starting for the Denver Whiz Bang, and playing alongside Ruth. McKenzie pitched a complete game, giving up only seven hits to the Denver Bears. Two came from Meusel.

After the game, Ruth attended a Knights of Columbus

banquet. He left Denver at some point to destinations unknown and did not reach New York until November 8th.

Meusel boarded a westbound train for sunny Los Angeles. He would be greeted by Edith, his bride of ten months. Long Bob would patrol the Yankee outfield with Babe until 1929, ending his 11-year big league career with the Cincinnati Reds. He retired in 1932 after two seasons in the minors.

Babe Ruth is a...Dad?

As the 1922 regular season ended, newspapers printed photos of "Mrs. Ruth" holding a sixteen-month-old baby girl. Little Dorothy, inheriting Babe's round face, clutches a small bat. She appears to be wistfully gazing toward center field. The caption noted she only weighed 2½ pounds at birth. People were "surprised" to learn Babe Ruth had a daughter. Ruth claimed they had been sheltering Dorothy from the public due to her delicate health.

Dorothy made her public debut at Fenway Park in Boston on September 26th, when the Yankees named her an "official mascot." (It was disclosed years later that little Dorothy had been adopted. Babe had fathered her with a mistress named Juanita Jennings. Dorothy only learned this at age 59.)

Often during the tour, Babe said he intended to keep a low profile once he got home. He and Helen were building a new house on a 78-acre wooded farm they owned near Sudbury, just west of Boston. Disappointed with his 1922 behavior and on-field performance, he vowed to be a good family man, chop piles of wood, and report to spring training in excellent condition.

Dorothy Ruth, the "Babe's" Baby

A picture of baby Dorothy Ruth with mom Helen appeared in papers during the barnstorming tour.

Photo courtesy of the *Olpe Optimist* (Olpe, Kansas), October 31, 1922

A New York Homecoming

Ruth arrived in New York on November 8th, ten days after his final game in Denver. Why it took him so long to travel home was not widely reported.

With a Big Apple welcome, the *New York Tribune* wrote that "...when he wasn't riding in Pullman cars, he was plowing around the infield of half-mile tracks at county fairgrounds, [where] most of the exhibition games were staged."

In another paper, Ruth admitted, "...we had a good time, though we didn't make as much money as expected." But without bad weather in Kansas City and Denver, he speculated, "...we could have come through 100 percent on the trip."

The afternoon following his return, he left his Ansonia Hotel suite to visit with Yankee co-owner Colonel Til Huston.

Club headquarters had temporarily moved to 226 West 42nd Street while construction on Yankee Stadium neared completion. Anticipating the appointment with Ruth, Huston lamented (perhaps tongue-in-cheek), "My goodness, can't be he needs money already?"

Following their meeting, Huston joined the New York press as the Bambino recalled his travels through the hinterlands. He explained that most games pitted the Yankee stars on opposing teams. Claiming they traversed the Great Plains unsupervised, he said, "…crowds were very kind to us, and newspapers in the West gave us a lot of attention."

The *New York Tribune* recounted the dialogue. Leaning against a door jamb, Ruth described "…long jumps between towns, sometimes 300 or 400 miles on a sleeper."

"We got as far west as Denver and as low down as sleeping all night on the floor of a day coach on a jerkwater railroad that made you think you were always falling down a flight of stairs." He blamed poor track maintenance on a lengthy railroad worker's strike.

"Sometimes we got off the train and had to ride 50 or 60 miles by auto…and then hop right out after the game over a range of mountains to make some other connection. Some of the engines could only run downhill, and a lot of the cars were running along on square wheels," he groused, *slightly* exaggerating.

He recalled playing in rainy Kansas City, noting, "…seven-thousand people stuck it out to watch us." While pitching late in the Monarchs game, Ruth claimed his right fielder had six fly-ball errors in one inning. "He tried to catch the ball with everything but his hands, which makes the trick difficult."

No wonder the press loved him.

But the *Brooklyn Standard-Union* wrote, "…rumors as to Ruth's financial standing aroused the ire of the swatsmith, who declared that it was no one's concern but his own." Ruth snapped "…we made enough money…to make the trip worth our while."

Asked about his bandaged right hand, Ruth said an old laceration had sliced open and gotten infected late in the tour. He said a surgeon had cleaned and lanced it the previous day and predicted it would be fully healed in a week.

Inflated Home Run Totals?

Depending on his audience—and when he was talking—Ruth claimed he hit 21 homers in 21 games, with Meusel hitting 11. To another reporter, it was 20 homers in 17 games.

According to newspaper accounts, they played in eighteen games (including a rain-shortened, two-inning game in Kansas City).

Papers record him hitting either seven or eight homers during those contests. It depends on whether you count a post-strikeout, extra pitch blast in Bartlesville. (Bill Jenkinson lists seven in his book, *The Year Babe Ruth Hit 104 Home Runs.*)

Meusel had six dingers.

Maybe the Bambino included warm-up homers in his

inflated totals. *This was an exhibition tour, right?* The bottom line—it doesn't really matter.

And who would be dumb enough to argue with Babe Ruth?

Babe Mounts the "Horrible Holstein"

Not long after his press conference, Babe Ruth made his rodeo debut.

A famous circus equestrian in the 1920s, May Wirth claimed she could ride anything on four legs. She was friends with Ringling Brothers attorney John Kelley (not the "dick" Jimmy Kelly, mentioned earlier). Kelley bragged that nobody could survive a ride on "Fannie," his two-ton Holstein bull. Wirth wanted to prove Kelley wrong, and a private party was arranged on Kelley's farm near Englewood, New Jersey.

Hours after his New York press conference, Babe and his wife Helen accepted a party invitation from Kelley—contingent on the understanding there would be no press. But news of the party reached an anonymous *New York Herald* reporter and several other newsmen.

A self-described "right-of-way man for Ringling Brothers," Frank Cook met the writers as they arrived, warning them the event "…may be a pretty messy affair." He claimed Fannie had killed several riders. "He may not have killed them outright, but there have been a number of queer-looking deaths around Englewood in the past five or six years, and there is no proof that Fannie…hadn't [had] something to do with it."

Continuing to hype the peril, Cook invited the reporters inside—only if they promised to "say nothing to anybody." Writers entered with trepidation. "They beheld, standing meekly…Fannie, the horrible Holstein bull."

Nearby, "Babe Ruth was sitting on one end of a see-saw, hurling twenty-five selected and beautiful girls skyward, one after another…Mrs. Ruth stood by applauding."

Minutes later, acclaimed horse rider May Wirth was thrown onto the unassuming bull by former Princeton football star Big Bill Edwards. "Fannie uttered a bellow and quivered before wagging his tail and taking on a most benevolent expression."

"Miss Wirth stood on her head on Fannie's spine," then did a little dance while atop his back. The "Horrible Holstein" seemed to enjoy it and "almost smiled."

The crowd goaded Ruth into mounting the killer bull. "The Babe vaulted over Fannie's horns and landed on the Holstein's neck. Fannie sniffed and looked annoyed, but that's all."

The Bambino did this despite his bandaged right hand.

Hours after Ruth claimed it was a reinjury while playing ball, Frank Cook told the *Herald* writer it happened on the train ride back to New York. "Just to amuse the porters, Babe agreed to roll the bones with them one night in the dining car. Babe had rolled the dominoes for a while, and then one of the porters, thinking to amuse the Babe, slipped him a pair of red-hot steel dice that had been roasting in the kitchen."

If Babe hadn't played baseball for ten days—but claimed he had just gotten the injury cleaned and lanced *the day before*—which version makes the most sense?

A Vow of Sobriety at His Farewell Party

On November 20th, the night before Babe headed for home in Sudbury, Massachusetts, his agent Christy Walsh arranged a send-off party at the New York Elks Club. He invited the Baseball Writers of America. As the evening progressed and liquor flowed, several guests chastised Ruth for having been a poor role model the previous summer.

As state senator Jimmy Walker berated him, Ruth sobbed. The future New York mayor scolded that "Babe's duty was to the dirty-faced boy who got his impression of the Bambino from what he read in the papers." As the party wound down, Babe made a surprising and 'sobering' announcement.

"I have listened to what old heads have said…when a man gets a reputation, it carries responsibility. I'm going to the farm tomorrow…to work my head off, and I *hope* a lot of my stomach." Draining his tumbler, Babe pledged there would be no more drinking until after the 1923 season. "If I don't make good on my promise, then I am a bum."

Babe carries a 300 pound log for firewood at their Sudbury, Mass., farmhouse.

Photo Credit: Wikimedia Commons

The House That Ruth Built

Babe arrived in New Orleans for spring training, his six-foot, two-inch frame supporting "a lean 205" after chopping wood all winter. He claimed to have embraced clean living and self-discipline as promised. Jane Leavy uncovered a slightly different story. Mert Haskell farmed next to Ruth, later telling the *Sudbury Town Crier* that he had been the axman. "I'd do all the work and he'd sit there and drink beer and talk to me," Haskell said.

After training camp broke, the Yankees worked their way north by playing exhibition games in Louisiana, Mississippi, Texas, Oklahoma, and Missouri.

On April 18, 1923, an awestruck 74,217 fans entered Yankee Stadium to witness the inaugural Opening Day in

"The House That Ruth Built." Another 30,000 were turned away. With three grandstand levels, it dwarfed every other big-league park.

That morning, Ruth allegedly said he'd give a year of his life to hit the first Yankee Stadium home run. He didn't have to wait long. In the third, Babe blasted a slow curve from Boston's Howard Ehmke twenty rows deep into the right-field bleachers.

In the next two games, he bashed three balls over 450 feet. But none left the Yankee Stadium diamond. The deepest left-center field was 500 feet, nearly 50 feet deeper than the spacious Polo Grounds in 1922. He settled for two triples and a double.

Had the original dimensions of old Yankee Stadium been a bit smaller, how many more career home runs would Ruth have hit? On the other hand, the friendly right-field dimensions gave left-handed sluggers like Babe Ruth (and later, Roger Maris) a big advantage.

An MVP Season and
World Championship, 1923

Ruth had a brilliant 1923 campaign; some argue it was his career best. He led the American League in homers, RBIs, and walks. He finished second in batting to Harry Heilmann, despite hitting .393!

The Yankees cruised to the World Series, finishing sixteen games ahead of Detroit. Playing the Giants for the third consecutive year, the Bronx Bombers finally prevailed in six games for their first World Series title. Babe capped an excellent season by being honored with his only American League MVP award.

A Globetrotting Barnstormer

Ruth barnstormed regularly for the remainder of his career. After the '23 Series, he toured Pennsylvania and New York. A West Coast jaunt followed in 1924. Three home runs in Des Moines highlighted his 1926 tour.

Babe continued barnstorming between 1927 and '29. He toured California again in 1931, then ventured to Hawaii in 1933.

After the 1934 season, Ruth joined an American all-star team (including Lou Gehrig, Jimmie Foxx, and Charlie Gehringer) for an Asian tour. They stopped briefly in Hawaii before spending November in Japan, playing eighteen games. Those exhibitions generated wide interest, resulting in the formation of a professional Japanese baseball league in 1936.

The Americans then played in Shanghai before sailing to the Philippines for three final games. Robert Fitts documented the historic tour in his 2012 book, *Banzai Babe Ruth: Baseball, Espionage, & Assassination During the 1934 Tour of Japan.*

Going Out in Style—and Into the Hall of Fame

Despite hitting .288 with 22 homers in 1934, the Yankees didn't renew Babe's contract. At age 40, he joined the Boston Braves. Ruth batted an anemic .181 in 28 games with the National Leaguers.

He hit only six home runs for the Braves. But departing with Ruthian flair, he blasted *three* in his final game at Pittsburgh on May 25, 1935. His last one sailed 540 feet over the right-field roof, hitting a house across from Forbes Field. In his book *The Year Babe Ruth Hit 104 Home Runs*, Bill Jenkinson lists the distances of every career homer the Bambino hit. Of his 714 regular season blasts, only one went further than 540 feet.

Babe retired, hoping in vain to be picked as a major league manager. But club owners all felt Ruth lacked the maturity and self-discipline to be entrusted with coaching their players. Considering everything he had done for baseball, the snub was soul-crushing. He fell into a depression that may have haunted him for the rest of his life.

But in 1936, the Baseball Hall of Fame opened in Cooperstown, New York. Their inaugural inductees were Walter Johnson, Ty Cobb, Honus Wagner, Christy Mathewson, and the larger-than-life George Herman Ruth.

Babe's Final Years

In 1940, the Shriners sponsored a ten-day "Babe Ruth School" in the Quad Cities of Iowa and Illinois. Ruth enlisted several other former players (including future Hall of Famer Rabbit Maranville) to conduct the training. Afterward, he held hitting exhibitions in western Iowa, including Rockwell City and Sioux City.

In late 1946, doctors discovered an inoperable, malignant tumor in Ruth's neck and skull. He became one of the first cancer patients to receive experimental chemotherapy and radiation at the same time. His treatment helped write medical history.

His health declined slowly but steadily. He died, age 53, on August 16, 1948.

Epilogue

It's stunning to think that in October 2022—exactly a century after his 1922 "small-town America tour"—Babe Ruth popped up yet again in baseball news.

On October 3, 2022, Aaron Judge of the Yankees hit his 62nd home run of the season. That broke the American League record set by Roger Maris in 1961. Maris had broken Babe's record of 60, set in 1927. That same day, Albert Pujols of the St. Louis Cardinals passed the Bambino for second place on the all-time career RBI list.

But 75 years after his passing, it's difficult to realize that many of Babe's legendary feats had yet to occur in 1922. Ahead was the glorious 1927 "Murderer's Row" season— the fabled "called shot" during the 1932 World Series against the Cubs—and the 1948 Yankee Stadium farewell address he delivered as he leaned against Bob Feller's bat.

In October 1922, Babe had been a major-leaguer for nine years. 1922 had been the first full year that he hadn't pitched.

In crowning legends, Babe Ruth in 1922 may well be classified as an Intermediate Rookie. He had 197 regular season career home runs when the 1922 tour started. That's respectable for the era but hardly eye-popping compared to the additional 517 homers he had yet to hit in his next 13 seasons.

Given that perspective, maybe we can forgive the poor attendance in Lincoln and any other city not challenged by the weather. Statistically, his pitching records had exceeded his burgeoning hitting ability. And potential ballgame attendees faced the same conflicts we have today—work schedules, babysitting, and balancing spending priorities against disposable income.

Despite that, lucky thousands endured dust devils, sleet, and wet bleachers in October 1922 to see Babe Ruth and Bob Meusel in their "jerkwater" communities. The Bambino played many exhibitions in years to come. But financial considerations largely steered him away from hinterlands like Perry and Sleepy Eye and Drumright.

At least Babe Ruth gave those folks some exciting memories that would last a lifetime. And thankfully, Len Youngman lived long enough to share his memories with *us*!